Josh — Continued Success!

WHAT OTHERS ARE SAYING ABOUT JACK KILLION AND

network:
all the time, everywhere with everybody

"Over more than 35 years as an entrepreneur, Jack went from being a self-described "neophyte" at developing relationships to being astute and very successful. He has paid his dues and has a wealth of knowledge on how to build new relationships, and take care of existing ones. Whether you're a CEO or just starting out, this book provides actionable tools for any working professional."
–Keith Ferrazzi, Author of the #1 NY Times Bestseller "Who's Got Your Back" and "Never Eat Alone"

"Networking is as natural and necessary to Jack Killion as is breathing. Although he has been successful at breeding horses and publishing magazines, those were hobbies and vocations. Networking is his passion. And, that comes out clearly in his book. "Network Everywhere, All the Time, With Everybody" is a must read for anyone interested in developing relationships, as are books by Julia Child and James Beard for anyone interested in the art of cooking. Jack goes into great detail about the "why" for constructing networks and the "how" including using events to create networking opportunities.

D1005080

1

Then there is the simple breakfast meeting to start off a day of networking that works well, too. It is all presented in a straightforward and clear way with the result that networking, which is necessary in all facets of life, becomes something comfortable and natural, so that the reader becomes really good at it and passionate about

–Andrew J. Rosman, Ph.D. CPA, Dean, Silberman College of Business, Fairleigh Dickinson University

"The ability to form strong relationships is one of the most crucial success factors in business, opening doors and getting you more than a seat at the table. Yet, for many, networking—and doing it well— remains a huge, missed opportunity to create opportunities. Everyone knows building connections is important, but navigating how to do it as a life and career enhancing skill is not always so intuitive. Jack Killion's "how-to" resource on why we all need to network and how to do it successfully is a great resource, giving readers a head-start in mastering this essential skill. It is chock full of practical yet powerful insights culled from his more than 40 years honing networking skills as an entrepreneur and advisor to some of the world's leading brands. This is a must-read—if you want to further your professional journey or enhance the connections you form in life."

–Anthony Campanelli, Partner, Deloitte

"Jack Killion's book should be required reading. Not only does he outline in clear terms how to build and sustain meaningful relationships, but he also demonstrates how those skills are essential to building a successful business and leading a full life.

A recent survey revealed that, more than any other skill, employers want their new hires to be able to work together productively in diverse teams. His book is an anecdote-filled inspiration for all of us to build and sustain the kind of strong interpersonal relationships with strangers and friends alike that are the foundation for a successful business and a full life.

Without overlooking the usefulness of virtual networking the book is especially important for college students and young professionals who are adept at building a directory of "friends" in a superficial way through text and social media sites but who are much less at ease with the complementary and essential skills of deep-rooted and long-lasting in-person networking.

As Killion points out, networking is one of those essential activities that we do naturally as children--like dancing and drawing fantastical pictures as if no one were looking over our shoulder--but a skill that takes more conscious effort as we grow older.

This book celebrates our fundamental nature as social beings and shows us how to build and sustain the strong relationships that are the foundation for a successful business and a full life.

Killion is the ultimate networker, and here he shares his secrets."

–Tori Haring-Smith, President, Washington & Jefferson College

"I know Jack has hit on an important subject which he recognizes is not formally taught.

My father was a salesman and he taught me to "get on the level" of another person so we will have a commonality. Using this technique, Jack is right, we must network everywhere, all the time, with everybody to develop winning friendships and working relationships.

My networking mantra is that it's better to give than receive, but what goes around comes around. I think Jack epitomizes this ethos and I think everybody who wants to be on the same level with Jack should read his book. I highly recommend it."

–Fred C. Klein, Esq., Managing Partner, Klein Zelman Rothermel Jacobs & Schess LLP. Co-Founder: Gotham City Networking, Inc.

"I have read a lot of books on personal development and practical business books. This one rises to the top among the best of class. It's an insightful and powerful book filled with real life examples and tactics for people of all ages to benefit."

Jack has achieved the ultimate academic pedigree, climbed the corporate ladder and succeeded the roller coaster of entrepreneurship, not once, but multiple times. That gives Jack a unique perspective and set of lenses through which he can clearly articulate his experiences, insights, and advice. Take the advice! Read the book, execute on it to change and improve your life, and then help someone else do the same.

As a serial entrepreneur and adjunct college professor who mentors and advises students, executives, entrepreneurs and companies, it has become clear how so many people are weak in networking. There is a huge need for this kind of book to provide a roadmap filled with real life scenarios and tactics on how to start, build, and maintain meaningful relationships to improve one's career, business and life.

If Jack had only written this book sooner, how readers' lives could have improved earlier. It's an authentic book on how to build and maintain a network and how to leverage your network to change and improve your career, life and business. Equally important, it tells you how you can make a positive impact on other people's lives.

Happy adventures reading this book."

–Mukesh M. Patel - Entrepreneur, Private Equity Principal, Attorney, Mentor-Advisor to Start-ups & Growth Ventures, Adjunct Professor, Rutgers B.S., Founder: icepiration.com & JuiceTank.com

"One thing I have learned from working on Wall Street for 25 + years is to network when you don't need it. Jack Killion is a master networker. His lifetime of experiences will guide you towards opportunities you never knew existed. Jack's tips will help craft your story so you can articulate it with confidence to anyone you speak with. If you want to reach your full potential in your career and life, start networking.

Read Jack's book and get started now, because if you wait to network until you need it, it's too late."

–Greg Eagan, Managing Director, Alpine Associates Management

"I have a copy of Jack's book in my IPad and will continue benefiting from it for the rest of my life.

It was my quest for building a short list of wise friends to consult with in life defining situations that brought me face to face with Jack. I was surfing a professional networking website and saw Jack's profile vigorously advocating the importance of networking for success in life and business. He was advocating that we all build a short list of wise friends who will be open to share their advice in life changing situations.

Our first meeting was very interesting. I was taking mental notes of all his comments.. It was my first meeting with Jack and he was unknowingly responding to some of my business-relations building questions when he said, "It takes about six to nine months to build a professional contact". He was calm and very realistic about the prospects of new networking endeavors. This was not only my first meeting with Jack but also my first exposure to a "professional networking approach". What I picked from Jack - my wise friend - is that it is one step at a time like building of a pyramid or a skyscraper-Rome was not built in a day. We can't build it in one day, but we should continue putting on new bricks whenever we get an opportunity."

–Muhammad Rafiuddin Shah - CTITF Office, Department of Political Affairs, United Nations

"Everyone should read Jack Killion's new book on networking. Parents will do their children a favor by giving Mr. Killion's book as a high school graduation gift, when they are old enough to be curious about how to be successful. I have had the pleasure of knowing Jack for almost 5 years. Of course, I met him through networking. As a businessman, I have always been adept at connecting with clients and customers, but Jack has taught me the true art of how to network effectively.

First and foremost, he is always interested in learning more about others than him telling them about himself. This book will help all readers open the door to a new world; a world built on creating and building relationships. The result will make life more fulfilling on a personal level and help secure new leads for any business endeavor. Mr. Killion's book will enrich your life and sow seeds for any company's growth as you learn from others and others learn from you."
–Richard R Shapiro, President, The Center For Client Retention

"Networking is briefly defined as 'the exchange of information or services among individuals or groups, specifically for : the cultivation of productive relationships for business'. However, missing in this characterization is the fact that no one takes the time to explain why it is so important; or when, where, and how to engage in networking. That is until Jack Killion, as he makes no assumptions and effectively coaches you in what works…and in what does not. This book mirrors his life. Read and learn."
–John W. Kennedy, Ph.D, Chief Executive Officer. NJMEP

"Jack Killion is passionate about networking and communicating with people. He enthusiastically practices what he preaches each and every day. As a business associate and friend, whenever I need a resource, the first person I think of is Jack. And he never disappoints--he always comes up with the right person from the vast network of useful and inspiring contacts he has developed over the years. For a long time, his friends have been encouraging him to write this book in his own inimitable style--it is direct, practical, and answers all of the "why" questions."

–Isobel Wayrick, Vice President, Mars International

"Kudos to Jack Killion for writing this book on Networking! In the book, Jack gives many examples based on his life experiences, which help make it easy to read and understand. There is no question that proper networking is the key to success in life. Jack makes an important point that "You need to do a great job of networking in order to make connections that can result in important new opportunities." Another interesting part of his book is that networking is not just for business opportunities, it is a way of life. You can network with people all of the time about all aspects of your life, and improve it. I recommend this book to anyone with an interest in improving their lives, those of their loved ones and of their friends."

–Raymond Vaccari, Director of the New Jersey Advanced Manufacturing Talent Network hosted at the NJ Institute of Technology and NJIT Adjunct Professor.

"The best clients come from networking and relationship building. Jack Killion does an outstanding job of showing how networking can uncover profitable business relationships and hidden opportunities."

–Jeff Beals, Award Winning Author of Self Marketing Power and Selling Saturdays

"Networking, the art of generosity. Killion is both the grandfather and the new thinker of networking. His book teaches us that networking is not about selling ourselves but rather about how we interact with each other in a generous way. Networking with the Killion Method is a way of interacting from the heart If you want to reach your full potential in your career and life, start networking which creates more meaningful connections and is essentially the art of networking. He gives us practical and tangible tools to become great givers of relationships so we can grow not only our own business but also help others grow theirs. The true art of working and living interconnected."
–Jeanette Bronee, Founder: Path for Life Self-Nourishment Center. Author

"Jack Killion's book, Network All the Time, Everywhere With Everybody, helped me realize that networking is a continuous opportunity (and adventure) for everyone. If you are curious about others, enjoy connecting the dots, interested in personal and professional growth, or just don't feel like eating alone, this book offers terrific tips to make the most out of a new connection. It is a quick and easy read and even offers an action plan."
–Diana Bald, Senior Managing Director, National Agency & Strategic Partnerships at Safeco.

"Jack Killion can make you salivate over the incredible power of networking. He will light your fuse, get you off your butt, and send you out to build a network of trusting, win-win relationships that will sustain your working career."
–Sims Wyeth, Founder – Sims Wyeth & Co. Consultant, Speaker, Author

"Jack Killion is a master networker and an inspiration for all of us who strive to achieve more in our business and personal lives. 'Network All the Time, Everywhere with Everybody' should be required reading for anyone seeking to achieve at a higher level. By presenting a myriad of proven networking strategies interwoven with his extraordinary life experience, Jack offers lessons for professional and personal growth that would be impossible to find elsewhere."
–Michael Zeldes, Senior Vice President, Hub International Northeast

"I wish I had met Jack earlier in my career to gain the wisdom he holds. I had not received networking training in either undergraduate or law school, so I had to seek perspectives people I came across. It took about 3 years to gain Jack's perspective, which was when I finally understood the value and necessity of networking. In addition, the skills I learned from Jack have allowed me to develop genuine and insightful relationships with people. In fact, the skills I learned from Jack are much more valuable than some of the classes I have taken in school. We live in a world of networks, and networking has become equally important to education. One bit of wisdom Jack shared with me was if you're not networking, then you're hurting your family. This resonated with me and is only a hint of Jack's wisdom."
–Jennifer Jedra, IP Attorney, Myers Wolin, LLC

Eagle Rock Partners Press
Published by Eagle Rock Partners Press
Long Valley, NJ 07853
(908) 507-9879

www.networkallthetime.com,

ISBN: 978-0-9966717-0-5

This book is designed to provide information on networking and careers. This information is provided and sold with the knowledge that the publisher and author do not offer any legal or other professional advice. In the case of a need for any such expertise consult with the appropriate professional. This book does not contain all information available on the subject. This book has not been created to be specific to any individual's or organizations' situation or needs. Every effort has been made to make this book as accurate as possible. This book should serve only as a general guide and not as the ultimate source of subject information. The author and publisher shall have no liability or responsibility to any person or entity regarding any loss or damage incurred, or alleged to have incurred, directly or indirectly, by the information contained in this book.

The NQ Pulse Survey is the exclusive property of Bluestone+Killion and may not be reproduced or used in any form without express written permission from the publisher.

net**work:**
all the time, everywhere with everybody
(Master Your Life & Career)

Contents

The World Before Social Media

You want to succeed. Like most of us, you want to have a successful career and earn significant money. You want to be successful finding your soul mate and raising a thriving family. You want your own life to be rich with boundless experiences. You want to have special friends. Ideally you would like to find ways to give back to others.

Simply put, constantly creating new opportunities through relationships you develop is the key to how successful your career and your life will be.

Your ability to generate a constant flow of professional and personal opportunities is directly tied to your networking and relationship development skills. Thriving is a contact sport!

If you work and become skilled at meeting people and building successful relationships, you will be astounded at how far you will go both personally and professionally. You will be amazed at how enriched your life will be and the profound positive impact you will have on your family and on those you care most about.

Developing strong, meaningful relationships through effective networking is how to create opportunities that get you to where you would like to be.

But uncovering opportunities is not enough. To benefit, you have to take action to capitalize on the opportunities you uncover.

Why Read This Book?

When I was about thirty, I started, for the first time, to realize and begin to learn how important networking and developing long-term successful relationships could be to my life.

Up to that point, I was basically clueless. I put almost no effort into developing these skills. I failed to spot countless unknown opportunities in every aspect of my life. I don't want you to do that. It wasn't until I resigned my last paycheck job to start my own company that it hit me. I was going to have to learn to be good at meeting people and building solid relationships, or I was going to fail. Being off on my own meant I had to develop my own opportunities rather than rely on others to make good things happen for me. Over time, my safety net and my biggest personal asset became my network of connections with quality people.

When I first set out on my own, I was actually petrified to reach out to people cold. However, I had little choice, since I did not have established relevant connections with whom to start building important relationships. It wasn't easy for me. I am sure much about networking is not easy for you.

Back in the early seventies, I started almost every day in New York's Grand Central Station using the pay phones to reach out to people I hoped to meet and possibly work with. My hands got clammy on every call. Often I actually felt relieved when people didn't pick up their phone. Frequently after three rings, I would hang up, somehow thinking I had accomplished something just by trying.

Before cell phones, e-mails, LinkedIn, Facebook, Twitter, and other easy ways to communicate, landline phones and snail mail were the only ways to reach people, other than in person. Since I did not have an office when I started my first entrepreneurial company, which was providing venture capital and advice to emerging companies, I was left primarily with pay phones.

Over the past forty years, I estimate conservatively that I have put the magic ten thousand hours into networking and creating important relationships that is generally considered the time investment required to be good at anything, whether it is being a Major League Baseball player, a concert pianist, an artist, a software developer (like Bill Gates), a hardware and new product developer (like Steve Jobs), or a top-flight networker. Malcolm Gladwell wrote about the concept of ten thousand hours to success in his brilliant book Outliers. But you can start to get benefits almost immediately from networking, even if you are just starting out. You will only get better as you put in the time.

Networking can be learned. Some doubt this. Many believe people are born either to be good or not good at it. That simply is not true.

I guarantee if you work at it and have fun learning to network and develop successful relationships, you will see amazing results professionally and personally. This is true regardless of your personal qualities. You don't have to be a back-slapping, hand-shaking sales type to be great at networking. Some of the quietest, most reserved people I know are terrific networkers. One core reason they excel is they like people. They enjoy getting to know them and finding ways to add value to their lives.

My goal is to write the must-read book on networking and relationship development—the one book that will provide the direction you need to enjoy and be skilled at it. I want this book to positively change your life.

The best networking-related book I have read so far is Keith Ferrazzi and Tahl Raz's Never Eat Alone that was published in 2005. I recommend it all the time to anyone looking to sharpen their own skills.

I know that networking should be taught in all of our schools but is not. I think it is as important as reading, writing, and arithmetic. It is the one skill that, when mastered, will drive the success of your entire life. If you don't work at honing these skills, your career will suffer. Your personal life will be much less than it can and should be, and you will be shortchanging your family members' lives.

The responsibility for developing these abilities is entirely yours. Don't expect anyone else to be pushing and prodding you to do the things I cover in this book. The ball is in your court! When you finish the book I welcome your feedback either via LinkedIn or by e-mail at **Jack@networkallthetime.com** or by phone **(908) 507-9879.**

Who Should Read This Book?

The book is primarily for working professionals and corporate leaders and entrepreneurs looking to solidify and accelerate their careers and have a bottom-line impact on their organizations and new ventures while enriching their professional, personal, and family lives.

The book also serves as a road map for organization leaders looking to attract and retain the best talent as part of an overall plan to drive profitable, sustainable business growth.

However, the book also is an important resource for almost anyone including executives in transition, stay-at-home parents, college and high school students looking to develop their early lives and careers, and parents looking for ideas to enhance their own lives and for helping to shape their kids' futures.

Basically, everyone can benefit from learning to do a better job networking and building relationships.

You generate opportunities through the relationships you establish throughout your life.

Feel free to share this book. Help spread the message.

Why I Am Writing This Book

This book has been in my head for a few years. There are a couple of reasons for writing it.

Introduction

First, I don't want you to waste many of your prime years like I did, failing to learn how to discover and capitalize on the amazing people, experiences, and opportunities you encounter. As I said earlier, I was clueless how important networking and relationship development skills are. Looking back over the first three decades of my life, I realize now how naive I was not to network and develop great relationships in my early years. I was totally oblivious to the networking concept and certainly did not make any real effort to do it.

In the core eighteen to thirty years of my early working life, I had unlimited opportunities to meet exceptional people with their enormous personal and professional upsides and their own incredible networks that I could have tapped into. In this twelve-year period, I did the following:

- Graduated from Yale with a BS in mechanical engineering

- Graduated with a master's degree from MIT's Sloan Business School

- Took additional courses at the Harvard "B" School

- Was recruited for a fascinating first job out of college in London working for Elliott Automation, a leading public UK technology company

- Came back to the United States when I was drafted into the US Army

- Then joined and worked successfully for a few years with McKinsey & Company, the world's top management consulting firm at the time (In my mind it still is the best)

I am embarrassed I never developed any ongoing, significant friendships and business relationships with any of the amazing people I met along the way in this twelve-year stretch. How incredibly inconceivable is that? But there were reasons why I blew all these opportunities, which I get into later when I write about the hurdles that people deal with when networking.

To be totally fair to myself, I have maintained and grown three early-life relationships. Dick Shurman is still a friend. He came to my fourth-birthday party. His father was our family doctor. Bill Boynton and I went together to grammar school in Essex Fells, New Jersey, and then high school in Caldwell. We have maintained our friendship. Best of all, I met my super wife, Judy Chapman, in high school, and we are still together six decades later. Along with our son, Jonathan, arriving on the scene thirty-two years ago, Judy is easily the best thing that ever happened to me.

Back then, the world was different. The need to network and grow relationships was not as obvious. Nobody talked about it. There were no networking events or networking groups per se. Networking could not be done as easily as you can do it today.

My parents came through the Great Depression with only eighth-grade educations. They had to work hard to accomplish anything. My dad was a tool and die maker. My mom worked for the Penn Central Railroad that went belly up many years ago before shifting to being a stay-at-home mom caring for me and my sister, Pat.

Money was always tight (a real blessing in my mind). Life was far simpler with limited air travel. There was no TV. We bought the first one when we lived in our town of Essex Fells. Fast-food restaurants really didn't exist other than White Castle, which is still one of my favorites, although I think they make a huge branding mistake calling their burgers "sliders." So we almost never went out to eat, and we certainly never had conversations about "networking," whatever that meant at the time.

Bet most of you can't even envision life in the forties and fifties without all the communication tools that we take for granted today.

While my public schooling was good, it certainly did not stack up against the private schools that most of my Yale classmates attended. I went to Yale University with a perceived and very real lack of a solid public high school education. I was a bit of a misfit as the son of blue-collar parents in that cloistered community at the time of kids with privileged backgrounds. I lacked real confidence.

I grew up when the economy was still primarily a manufacturing one. In America we made things. People worked in factories in closely structured jobs. Factories produced products that were sold mostly to US customers. There was no outsourcing, limited importing and exporting, and almost no competition from lower-cost-producing nations.

For the most part, the products that we did import were of poor quality and not much of a competitive threat to US manufacturers. In the manufacturing era, companies succeeded or failed primarily based on the performance and need for their unique products.

In today's service economy, many services provided by similar organizations competing for the same clients look and are similar. One tax return or audit looks much like any other. The lending terms and conditions from one bank to another vary little. In today's service economy, it is much more difficult to assess differences among the work done by similar service providers. Today, professionals have to rely heavily on relationships they develop with their clients as the glue that binds client and service provider together. This doesn't happen if you don't have terrific "people skills."

Skilled networking is definitely one of the keys for the success of many thousands of organizations in all sectors.

If I were heading a service company today, such as an accounting or law firm, investment advisory firm, a bank or consulting firm, I would, for sure, make certain our people, all of them, were learning to be exceptional networkers and relationship developers.

But I digress. In the forties and fifties, public transportation was limited. People sometimes could commute locally by trolley or bus. International travel was rare. Domestic air travel was just getting off the ground (pun not intended). People got their news primarily from daily newspapers and the radio. For entertainment, they bowled, went to the movies, read magazines like LIFE, LOOK, Reader's Digest, and the Saturday Evening Post. They read books or jumped in the car and "took a ride."

Getting into college was not as tough as it is today with the current influx of applicants from around the globe trying to get into our better universities. Stanford in 2014 admitted about five percent of its applicants! Other best-in-breed American universities had similarly low admissions rates in 2014 and 2015. Generally, if you were set on attending a good college or university and had decent grades, you could anticipate being admitted to one of your top choices.

Milk, when I was a kid, was delivered to the home by a milkman and his dependable horse and wagon. That was one job my wife's father had along with having his own lawn care and custodial businesses.

The post–World War II economy was booming. People had relative job security. Millions of people actually worked for only one company their entire lives. Most people saw no need to network and develop a robust group of relationships.

Those days, of course, are basically over and won't be coming back. Job security is a thing of the past, even for most union, government, and postal workers. The majority of people will have six, seven, or even more careers, many often demanding new skills.

Today we all have to constantly reinvent ourselves by developing a continuous flow of new potential opportunities from the relationships we cultivate.

We live in an intensely competitive global economy with instant communication. Everyone with a laptop or a mobile phone or device can comment on anybody or anything and compete with anybody, anyplace, anytime.

The family unit was stronger years ago. America did not have a fifty percent divorce rate. Teen pregnancies were not rampant. Drugs were not widespread. Fewer people owned guns and the ones they did own were not AK15s. Politicians were generally polite to each other and often tried to work together. Hard to imagine isn't it?

The pace of living today is incredibly fast. The ability to go it alone is almost nonexistent. To thrive you have to network. You have to forge strong relationships. You have to be constantly turning up new opportunities and deciding which ones to act on.

Most important of all, you have to take action when opportunities are uncovered.

The second reason for writing this book is now I have things to share with you. I paid my dues.

During the past several decades, I went from being a total neophyte at networking and relationship development to being an astute, successful, and effective networker. Many of the people in my circle think I am among the best networkers they know. That may not be saying much since so few people really do work to develop these abilities. Nevertheless, I have clearly turned myself into a networking machine and benefit from it enormously.

Since quitting my last job over forty years ago with McKinsey & Company, I have been living the entrepreneur's choppy, volatile life with a series of ventures from being in the earliest stages of venture capital to book and magazine publishing to manufacturing industrial equipment to breeding and training race horses to real estate development in Florida to investment services to coaching executives and professionals to network.

Over the years I:

- Started six different businesses

- Bought and grew two other businesses

- Helped my wife, Judy, start her Garden State Woman publishing and events company and her nonprofit Garden State Woman Education Foundation

- Advised the founders and owners of hundreds of other businesses

There is more about my background at the end of the book, if you have an interest.

If I had not forced myself to sharpen my skills at networking and building successful relationships, I never could have survived the past forty years of living and working on the entrepreneurial edge.

When I started improving these skills, personally I was faced with all of the challenges that may currently inhibit you and others from getting out there, talking to people, attending events, joining groups, finding ways to help, staying in touch, and building long-term viable relationships.

I had no alternative but to learn how to network. That was the only way I was going to create opportunities, get input on my thinking, win clients for my efforts, and attract people to join my team. I taught myself to network without ever realizing what I was doing or labeling my efforts as such.

In decades of networking, I have met amazing people. For example, I have been to the White House three times. When younger, I found two job opportunities outside the United States, first in France and then in the UK. I have been referred to astonishing places around the world, learned to raise funding for projects, generated rapidly growing profits primarily by leaning on my network of special connections, and had great fun and excitement building and tapping into my network.

I have helped my wife and son hone their networking skills and realize their own important benefits as a result.

So I am writing this book to encourage you to ramp up your own networking and relationship development efforts starting today, regardless of how good or bad your skills may currently be. Improving these critical skills needs to be a lifetime process. We all can get better at doing it. I get better at it every day.

In this book, I share my considerable networking thinking, observations, lessons learned, and efforts with you. The book covers a lot that will benefit you.

Everybody, regardless of any other factor in their lives, can develop exceptional networking abilities, which, in the long run, are likely to be the single biggest factor in determining the quality of your career and the life you and your family enjoy. Age is certainly not a deterrent to developing these abilities.

This book will motivate and provide you with actionable tools enabling you to take your networking and relationship development skills to a still higher level and accomplish much more than I ever have. Enjoy the journey!

Chapter One

The Basics:
Casting the Net to Catch the Big Fish
(and Little Ones Too)

To me, our network of win-win relationships is the single most important asset any of us can have outside of our families.

There isn't any need to get too complicated defining what I mean by networking. It means simply meeting lots of people, staying in touch with some of them, and working hard to develop long-term, successful relationships with many that benefit you both personally or professionally.

The quality of your network will generally determine the quality of every aspect of your life. It will determine if you are in charge and driving your life or if your life and your family's lives are being dictated by others.

In this book I will simply use networking most of the time when I mean it includes relationship development. That's the point of networking. Networking is the means to an end, not the end itself. You need to do a great job of networking in order to make connections that can result in important new opportunities.

The cycle you need to think about is to meet people by networking, build win-win relationships, generate a constant flow of potential opportunities, and then act to capitalize on the best of these opportunities.

The Networking Cycle

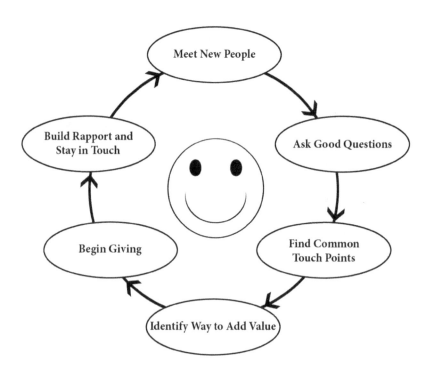

Today effective networking certainly means both encounters in person and using social media, which did not exist even ten years ago.

Interestingly enough, the word networking combines two words that apply. A net is a system of connections whether a computer network, a basketball net, a spider web, or a personal one. When we talk about networking, we really are focusing on developing a relevant and important net of our personal and business connections.

The word work also applies when thinking about and actively putting effort into successful networking. Successful networking requires real effort to overcome our personal challenges to being good at it, to find time to do it the right way, and to develop the skills and knowledge required to be successful at it. Effective networking takes consistent effort, patience, and use of both time and money if you are to realize substantial benefits.

Why Is Networking So Important?

An article in the MIT Sloan Management Review ("The Social Side of Performance") says, "What really distinguishes high performers from the rest of the pack is their ability to maintain and leverage personal networks. The most effective create and tap large diversified networks that are rich in experience and span all organizational boundaries."

Authors Anne Baber and Lynne Wayman in their American Society for Training & Development article, "The Connected Employee," refer to a point made in "Developing Business Leaders for 2010," a report from the Conference Board, that said, "One of the four key essential leadership roles is relationship/network builder."

We live and compete on a global basis with our personal and professional successes tied directly to the quality of our individual networks and our skills in interacting with those in our networks or clusters.

The world has always been more than any of us could handle by ourselves. That's why early mankind grouped themselves together in tribes and clans. Then, as civilization evolved, we developed villages, neighborhoods, towns, cities, states, and countries. Then we linked these clusters of people together with other clusters in other parts of the world. Clearly in the early centuries, none of this was easily accomplished, given challenging, formidable travel and communication barriers.

We now live in a world where international and eventually interplanetary travel and near instantaneous communication are possible. However, now more than ever, it is vital that we each develop and learn to use our personal networks both belly-to-belly and via evolving social media technologies.

To a large extent, our ability to grow and harvest our robust and relevant networks will directly impact the:

- Careers we develop

- Incomes we earn

- Value we have to our employers

- Richness of our personal and our family lives

- Our ability to give back to others

Most people who have not really thought about networking often think that the major reason to do it is to achieve some sort of short-term business-oriented benefit—that is, many equate networking to selling, which means landing another order from an existing customer or attracting a new customer or signing another longer-term agreement.

To me, networking is much more life and career changing than that, with benefits coming in four different ways as shown here:

There Are Four Benefits From Successful Networking

Create Opportunities for Your Company	**Accelerate Your Own Career**
Enrich Your Family and Friends' Lives	**Enhance Your Own Life**

Interning One Summer in Tarare, France, Taught Me How Critical Networking Is

Following my freshman year at Yale, my dad was able to get me a paid summer internship working for a small, family-owned polymer processing company in Tarare, France. The company manufactured plastic floor and wall coverings.

I was uneasy going, having never been on a commercial airplane before. My dad owned a Cessna 172, which I soloed while in high school. So flying was not a new experience. However, flying internationally was. Besides this being a trip outside the United States, I had never studied French and was heading to a small village (at the time) where nobody other than the business owner spoke English. His English wasn't great.

This could be a long story, but I will keep it short to illustrate a point. Three people from the company picked me up in Paris the day I arrived and drove at an average speed above one hundred miles per hour to the company in Tarare, 365 km and several hours away. I didn't understand a word they said. In Tarare they arranged for me to rent a room from a villager, an older widow who could use the rental income.

31

She spoke no English.

There was basically one restaurant in town where I and the other residents ate all our meals. There were no menus. People just ordered from the selections they described each day. That restaurant is the first place I ate snails (love them now) and rabbit (not sure about that still) and drank café au lait, which, when served with real French bread, is the best!

There was no public transportation, so I walked to and from work every day, passing the restaurant on the way along the more than two-mile hike each way. Most employees biked.

The owner of the business traveled most of the time, which meant, when he was gone, I could not speak English with anyone in town or at the company. I had to learn French and learn it fast or I was going to be one miserable puppy for the summer. Rosetta Stone didn't exist. Obviously, there were not any tutors. Everything in writing was in French. So that particular summer, I learned where networking stacked up versus reading, writing, and arithmetic. It was my numero uno priority.

I just had to force myself to communicate using hand signals, slow simple English, and my slowly evolving French with as many people as possible every day and in all situations. The book title says it all: I was networking all the time, everywhere with everybody. Within a few weeks, I could start to communicate "okay" with people, although the villagers and company workers generally still laughed at me.

By the end of the summer, I was sharing a cottage with two younger managers from the company. It was often hard for people to imagine I was an American. I was quite fluent in French. One of the better aspects of this story is that when my cousin John Hall was in college many years later, I was able to network him to an internship with the same company.

If I could network successfully among people who could not speak English in a French town of a few thousand people, you can certainly learn to network more effectively in your circumstances.

If this is the only message you take away from this book, then writing it will have been worth the effort. Too many people, maybe the majority, simply don't "get it" when it comes time to think about and work on their networking and relationship development abilities.

The "don't get its" think networking is shallow. It's selling. It's trivial. It's all about getting versus giving, and it is a waste of time that interferes with their other priorities. How wrong they are.

Who Does and Who Should Network?

Let's get right to the bottom line. Basically I think everyone should network, and to varying degrees, we all do. There really is not any way to avoid doing some networking, regardless of our life situations.

We are born into our first network—our family. That's when we first start learning to meet new people and develop long-term, hopefully win-win, trust-based relationships.

Little kids certainly network when they go to day care and kindergarten, go to birthday parties, have sleepovers, join the scouts, go to camps, and go to Sunday school or their temple. All these activities create networking opportunities that most of us take advantage of for a few years with the early friendships we develop.

When we get into our high school and college years, again we network via the relationships we create in our classes, with our teachers and professors, in the clubs we join, on the class trips we take, on the school and traveling teams we join, and with our various activities during summers and other break periods. Some of us, meaning the ones who "get it," hang onto the most valued of these early-life friendships for decades. I was never that smart, which bothers me today.

As we get out into the workforce, get married, have kids, and get involved in our communities, we again have incredible networking opportunities and experiences with colleagues, customers, suppliers, advisors, neighbors, members of our various tennis, golf, and community clubs, parents of our kids, and the list goes on.

In the later years, we still have the opportunity to maintain and grow previous relationships as well as forge new friendships and strong relationships with the advisors we picked to guide us in retirement.

The point is, I do not see why learning to be a successful networker and relationship developer cannot enrich our lives almost from the day we are born until our last day on planet Earth. Do you agree?

Certainly I feel strongly that high school kids should be sharpening their networking and relationship skills, skills that they should hone, use, and benefit from for the rest of their lives.

Just to drive the point home with some specific examples:

• High school kids should network in order to create opportunities that will enhance their backgrounds so that they are the strongest possible candidates when it comes time to apply to colleges of their choice or to seek their first jobs. For the past fifteen years, I have interviewed quality high school students applying to MIT. Almost without exception, they all have outstanding grades and maybe half have perfect SAT scores. Too few have capitalized on their contacts and their family contacts to spot and pursue unique opportunities in their schools and their communities that help them build a robust resume that will appeal to top universities.

• College students obviously should be networking throughout their four years in order to line up important internships that can lead to full-time job offers following graduation. Today, too many young people are leaving college, many thousands of dollars in debt with student loans and lacking viable job prospects and no real sense of how to develop their own initial career opportunities. They can easily remain either underemployed or unemployed for a year or longer.

• While still in college is when young people have access to important potential contacts through the alumni group, professors, other students, their families, and other clusters of their contacts. Failing to build and harvest these contacts is a critical mistake too many college students make.

• Obviously anyone unemployed or underemployed or unhappy where they are working should be putting serious effort into networking and triggering new relationships. In few cases, maybe less than five to ten percent, will the next career move come from answering an ad or from one of the online search sites such as Monster.com or TheLadders.com. The majority of jobs being filled, maybe as high as seventy-five percent, come directly from referrals either from people already working within an organization or from those with contacts within that organization. Many new job openings are never posted anywhere. They get filled primarily through appropriate referrals.

• Anyone out of work and searching for another, better opportunity needs to view networking as their current job. If they are not out mixing it up with relevant people eight to ten hours every day, they are likely to be "toast" for a long time.

• Obviously the older you get and find yourself needing a new opportunity, the tougher it will be to find another chance and the harder you need to work at building and harvesting your high-potential network.

• Those in the early years of their careers need to be consistently building and using their networks. It's rare that anyone stays with one or two organizations throughout a lifetime of work. Now the norm is to have multiple employments over the span of a career. Economists are forecasting a global shortage of skilled workers. They expect millions of people to work at various jobs simultaneously to help solve the talent gap.

I learned recently that the average age of people working in New Jersey manufacturing jobs is over fifty-five. Manufacturing demand is coming back in the United States, but, for the most part, companies in the sector cannot find the new manufacturing-trained talent they need. It is a big problem for America.

The best way to maximize the number of your future opportunities is to spend plenty of time meeting and developing effective long-term relationships with quality people along the way.

C-level executives (CEO, COO, CFO, and other "chiefs") in all types of organizations are expected to be the driving rainmakers in their organizations. Having already excellent networking and relationship development skills is for sure one of the factors that likely supported their run to the top. But once they are on top, their need to excel with these skills is even more important as the leaders look to have the organization internally develop the next group of future leaders, create new strategic alliances, develop and launch new products and services, and penetrate new vertical niche and global markets.

We have all heard about the glass ceiling that women often feel they hit in their careers. I see another "ceiling" that both men and women can hit as they try to move up. I call it the "skills ceiling."

Having strong technical skills is no longer enough to set you apart from the herd and get you high up the career food chain. Assume millions of others have equally strong technical skills compared to yours. Be assured you are valuable to your organization. Be equally assured you can be replaced. You are not in control of your future if you are relying primarily on a strong skill set to drive your career.

To develop your career, earn more money, and take much more effective control of your future, you need to be a "difference maker"—that is, a serious rainmaker.

Being a difference maker means you have a robust network of relevant and important relationships that you developed over the years and that you can tap into and create new opportunities for your organization. Can you claim you can do this? Are you a difference maker? Are you hard to replace?

**Difference Making Rainmakers
Break Through the Skills Ceiling**

Rainmakers combine strong networking and relationship development skills with their technical abilities. They have great value to their organizations and are hard to replace.

**The
Skills
Ceiling** ────────────────────────────

"Good" Performers Rely on Technical Abilities

They struggle breaking through the skills ceiling. They do good work but lack networking and relationship development skill and do not make a real difference.

Business owners, if they hope to succeed, have no choice but to become exceptional networkers and relationship developers. I spent years raising money for and providing strategic guidance to owners and operators of emerging companies. I know their challenges in starting and growing a successful venture.

Too many business owners and leaders think that networking is mostly about collecting business cards at events and trying to generate new sales. The payoff from exceptional networking will impact every aspect of a business including:

- Recruiting new talent

- Finding better suppliers

- Developing new products and services

- Attracting strong advisors

- Raising growth funding

- Finding acquisition targets

- Finding potential buyers as an exit strategy

- Penetrating new markets

- Monitoring competition

One of the points I always make to people considering starting their own company is this: don't do it if you are at all reluctant to meet new people and be the out-front person in your company responsible for personally driving the sales and profitable growth of the business. Translation: If you own the business, you better be happy and skilled selling. This means you better know how to network effectively and create substantial relationships.

The obvious need for all of us to continue daily to sharpen and use our networking and relationship development skills is clear for anyone thinking about their future, even just a little.

Effective networking is not restricted to the good guys. Even bad guys network. The terrorists who attacked us on 9/11 and at our embassy in Beirut and elsewhere around the world certainly taught themselves how to network. They know how to develop fruit-bearing relationships that can devastate the rest of us. Often these relationships are accomplished without ever meeting each other in person. The Internet has facilitated terrorists including ISIS banding together in global networks, all easily cobbled together into a huge unseen and largely untraceable Internet-based network.

The vicious Mexican, Columbian, and other drug cartels all network successfully within their own groups and with other groups internationally.

In America the Crips, the Bloods and hundreds of other street gangs know how to network with their members—both those on the street and those in prison. Clearly they know how to identify the people they want in their networks. They know how to form long-term relationships that will get the gang to where they want to go.

I bet many of the professionals and corporate execs with their Ivy League degrees could learn a thing or two about the keys to effective networking from the "bad" guys. I am sure I could learn a lot as well.

With Whom to Network?

I think the basic first step to being a successful, results-producing networker is to talk with everyone you meet. That's with whom I think you should initiate your networking efforts.

Go through every day talking with as many people as possible without disrupting your life. Adopt the attitude of "let's talk."

From a purely career and business point of view, you need to be networking and building win-win relationships both externally and internally within the organization where you work. In some cases, particularly in professional firms such as accounting, legal, financial services, consulting and banking, corporations, and charities and government agencies, your internal network may be even more important to your long-term personal and career success than your external connections.

It is obvious that the lack of internal networking and relationship development at all levels in major professional firms and diversified corporations limits cross selling and cross referring. As a result, growth of the organization is stunted. Silos in organizations are killers. They limit cross selling, innovation, and team and people development. Virtually every major organization I know is being seriously held back by their formal or informal "silo structure" culture. See a later chapter for some of my thoughts on the relationship between networking and culture.

People are for the most part fascinating creatures if you take even just a little time to discover them.

I get a lot of enjoyment simply by talking with everyone, everywhere, at any time. This doesn't mean changing my lifestyle in any way or making any special effort to reach out to strangers. But it is amazing how much you can learn talking to someone standing or sitting next to you on a subway, waiting in the checkout line in the food store, standing next to you at one of your son's or daughter's games or activities, or chatting in the theater during intermission or at the baseball or football game or at a wedding, bar or bat mitzvah or even at a funeral.

Networking at the Food Store

I was stuffing my wife's free Garden State Woman magazine in a rack we had in a local supermarket. That's how I spent my Saturdays, filling racks with complimentary copies in twenty-eight food stores throughout northern New Jersey. Ugh! A woman asked if she could have a copy. What caught my attention immediately was her amazing accent, which I just had to ask about.

It turned out she was raised in South Africa, which naturally led me to ask what she was doing food shopping in Morristown, New Jersey. She told me that she was heading the entrepreneurial studies program at Fairleigh Dickinson University, which was just down the road. I told her I was an entrepreneur with experiences in many business sectors and had previously taught as an adjunct professor in the MBA programs at

Rutgers and Montclair State universities.

I asked if we could meet for coffee one morning to discuss if there might be an opportunity for me to get involved as an adjunct at Fairleigh Dickinson.

Over ten years later, I am still involved in multiple ways with the University. It all resulted from taking the initiative to strike up a conversation with an interesting person I met randomly at the local market. "Hi, you have an amazing accent. Where are you from and why are you here?" The total conversation probably lasted no more than three minutes, but it has led to a ten-year-plus friendship.

Nothing says that you have to stay in touch with people you talk to randomly, but simply by reaching out to people, you will certainly come across a few with whom you do want to nurture a longer-term friendship and possibly a business relationship. This has happened too many times for me to even mention, although I will give a few examples as we move through the book together.

The point is, start talking with as many people as possible and see where that leads you. Practice makes perfect. You can develop a lot of networking-related confidence and comfort simply by talking to all the people you meet just getting through your daily routine. Building up your confidence and skill level with these low-hanging-fruit connections will set you up when you need or have opportunity to meet and develop relationships with the big hitters.

By accepting it is a good thing to talk with virtually everyone you meet, many of the new relationships you start to develop will cut through various parts of your life. Random (I call it serendipitous) networking is good for this.

Planned networking in our "clusters" and targeted networking are also efforts that almost all of us should focus on to uncover the life- and career-changing opportunities we all seek.

Where to Network?

Network everywhere, all the time, with everybody. It's as simple as that.

Anytime you are in the company of other people, start networking. Remember this is a "game" where practice does make perfect. So get comfortable talking/networking with people everywhere including these opportunities:

• Waiting in the doctor's office: *Hi, how long have you been using this doctor?*

• Standing in your local food store checkout line: *Hi, I have never tried that brand yogurt. Is it your favorite?*

• Sitting next to you on a bus, train, or plane: *That looks like an interesting book you are reading. What is it about?*

• Sitting next to another couple in a restaurant: *Hi, that looks great. Would you mind telling me what you ordered?*

• Waiting in line to buy tickets to the movies, a play, or a game: *I have heard great things about this play. Have you?*

• At one of your kid's events at school: *Our son has enjoyed practicing for this. Have you heard the same thing from your son or daughter?*

• Staffing the reception desk at an organization you are visiting: *You seem to enjoy your job. What makes this company so good to work with?*

• Sitting in your company's waiting room when you get back from lunch: *Is someone helping you? Who are you here to see? What do you do? How can I help?*

The message is clear. Start talking. You can never tell where the conversation will lead. Maybe nowhere, but it doesn't take any real effort to show a genuine interest in others.

Missed Networking Opportunities at the New York Marathon

A good friend ran in the 2013 New York Marathon along with about forty thousand others. He was telling me about the amazing people he met both during the five hours between when he registered and the time he actually started to run and then during the run/walk itself.

Before starting to run, he collected many names of people also waiting to get started and their contact data on his iPhone. But because his battery ran out partway into the race, he did not have the ability to continue collecting names that way. I asked him if he brought his business cards with him. He said no and realized then he obviously lost some opportunity to stay connected with people he met along the way running and walking, both participants and those on the side cheering the marathoners on. All he needed was a little fanny pack to hold his cards, which he could have handed out along the way. Maybe nobody would have followed up with him. But maybe a few would have.

Network Internally

One point I want to emphasize is to network internally as well as externally. By internally networking, I mean within the organizations in which you spend the bulk of your work time.

I learned this lesson very early on while working with McKinsey

& Company. In my role as a strategic management consultant to leaders of major organizations, such as American Express, Burlington Great Northern Railway, Port of Philadelphia, Columbia Records, City of New York and more, I clearly had my "outside" client organizations within which to network and build viable relationships. Some of these client relationships led to my receiving potentially interesting job opportunities with their organizations.

Often whether or not McKinsey continued to get new assignments from my clients was heavily a function of the quality and depth of the relationships I developed with the client's senior management team. I and all the other associates at McKinsey were really the faces of the firm with the clients. How well we performed as consultants and how strongly the client relationships we developed could directly foster or kill a valued and important McKinsey-client relationship.

Very quickly I realized, however, that I also needed to network internally within the McKinsey & Company organization including in the New York headquarters as well as with leaders in other McKinsey offices around the country and the globe. I understood that my future with McKinsey in terms of compensation, promotions, teams I was assigned to and the nature of the projects I got to work on were all tied directly to the quality of the internal network I created for myself. I needed my champions internally.

It was clear I had two set of equally important (to my future) clients: the key people within the organizations I consulted with and leaders within McKinsey & Company.

Effective Internal Networking at College

Recently I was having breakfast with my good friend Ken who shared a story reflecting on the importance of internal networking. One of Ken's friend's sons was attending Villanova and, as a senior, was looking for his first career opportunity. He had set his heart on working with a major Wall Street firm like Morgan Stanley or Goldman Sachs. His primary offer at the time was from PNC, a quality bank.

So he started networking within the Villanova community asking other students if they had parents working at any of his target firms. He found many did, so he asked if they would be willing to connect him with them during the next parents' weekend.

To make a long story short, he quickly used these connections to get the necessary interviews and wound up with three job offers from exactly the quality and type of organization he wanted to join. He learned to network within his organization, which was Villanova University.

I am appalled at how little networking goes on internally within most of the major organizations with which I come into contact. To have some fun one day, pay attention when you are in a large organization how many people pass each other in the halls without either looking at each other or saying hi. It blows my mind.

Are you paying attention to building your own internal networks?

Benefits of Networking

Don't view networking narrowly. Successful networking doesn't only mean landing your next great job or another major client or another large order or another key strategic alliance. I appreciate all the business benefits I get from networking—the big ones as well as the small ones.

I have certainly networked my way to buying companies, raising important amounts of money for projects I was pursuing, landing key new clients, and getting the million-dollar order and more.

Equally important from a quality-of-life vantage point, we have used effective networking to help my wife, Judy, grow her Garden State Woman (gswoman.com) business and her nonprofit and to help our son, Jonathan, get his first two jobs out of college. Both were with major organizations where he learned a lot, made great connections, took on major responsibilities, and was well paid for his efforts.

At age thirty-two, he is on a fast track career-wise with a balanced, full personal life. He has learned to live to the fullest, leaning heavily on his network to develop important lifetime business friendships and working relationships and to find the special places in and outside the United States to visit, scuba dive, play golf, ski, enjoy, and more.

Recently Jonathan and his awesome girlfriend, Emily, spent ten days in Peru; four days were spent hiking the trail to the Machu Picchu ruins in the Andes. Given it was his first trip to Peru, he had little idea of how best to spend the balance of the trip. So he did what comes naturally to him now. He Googled to see if there was a Georgetown University Club in Peru. DC-based Georgetown is where he went to college to study accounting and finance.

He found an alumni club in Lima. He reached out via e-mail to the club president who was thrilled to hear from another Hoya graduate. She arranged for Jonathan and Emily to meet six other alums one night for dinner in Lima. From the group he learned all the special places to visit during his trip to the country.

Over the years, our family learned, through networking, about great recipes, wines, restaurants, get-away vacation spots, movies, plays, books, special-interest magazines, places to shop, places to live, breeders to buy thoroughbred horses and different dogs from and much more. Our lives are robust from the depth of the network we developed and the abilities we honed to harvest our networks.

Networking benefits, both personal and professional, obviously vary from person to person but always have the potential to impact your life in four ways:

- Help accelerate your career either where you currently work or in new opportunities that skilled networking will uncover for you.
- Increase your value to your current employer. In this era of low to no job security, you certainly want to be perceived as having real substantial value for your organization. One of the obvious ways to have real value is by developing and working with contacts in your robust professional network. The more positive revenue- and profit-generating relationships you can create for your organization, the greater your value will be to the organization.

- Enhance your personal life by steering you to all the resources that you value and can positively impact your life. Networking will uncover restaurants you should try, books you should read, movies and plays you should see. Networking is how you will find the right advisors you need to guide your financial future and how you will learn about U.S. and international getaways.

If you live an introverted, noninvolved personal and professional life, you are clearly going to miss out on many of life's best experiences. You may in fact struggle your entire life, never being in control of things happening to you. You may never grasp the penalty you pay for not developing and harvesting your network.

In this intensely competitive world, your network really becomes the most important part of your overall net worth. It's where you can turn to when you hit roadblocks and hurdles. It's where you find your next unique personal and/or business opportunity.

- Enrich your family's life. Networking will be the way you learn about the communities to live in, the schools your kids would enjoy and benefit from vacation spots to try, groups and clubs to join, and nonprofits to give back to. Networking will help your family make the right college choices for your kids and can turn up summer internship and full-time early-career jobs that get them off to a fast start.

If you are not actively growing your network of quality contacts, there is no doubt that you are shortchanging yourself and, equally important, shortchanging your family.

In my own case, just a few of the many ways I have benefited include:

• Getting into Yale University partially based on my high school English teacher really going to bat for me with her strong recommendation to her Yale connection

• Landing a paid summer job in France while still in college based on a connection my dad had developed over the years with the French business owner

• Getting my first job out of MIT Sloan's Business School with a high-tech UK-based company on the recommendation of a YPO member (Young Presidents' Organization) with whom I had worked one summer in New Hampshire

• Attracting two partners to join me in a new company I formed to provide fundraising and management direction to high-potential emerging companies (I met both as clients when I was consulting while at McKinsey & Company.)

• Finding a boutique European hotel to stay at in Paris with my family, a recommendation from a friend who had stayed at the same place two or three years earlier

• Deciding to take our son to Tortola in the British Virgin Islands to scuba dive based on the recommendation of a good friend who had been there many times (I knew zero about the British Virgin Islands before reaching out for some guidance.)

• Helping our son land his first job out of Georgetown University. My wife had a high-level connection with Deloitte, one of the world's premier accounting firms (Her contact certainly didn't guarantee Jonathan a job. But it did create an opportunity for him to be looked at seriously. He started with them within two weeks of graduating from college. How many college graduates today would appreciate a connection like that on their parent's part?)

• Attracting serious long-term investors to my fourteen-year-old Eagle Rock Diversified Fund that I launched in 2001 (Every investor in the fund has been referred in by someone I know and who knows me well.)

• Forming a new company (In 2012 a longtime friend, Andy Bluestone, sat in on a networking training seminar I ran for fifty professional and corporate women readers of my wife's Garden State Woman magazine. A few days after the three-hour workshop, Andy suggested there was an opportunity for us to form a new training firm to coach others how to network and build important relationships. That's the background behind Bluestone+Killion (bluestonekillion.com).

Fortunately my list of specific tangible benefits resulting from my networking efforts as well as from Judy's and Jonathan's networking efforts could fill the rest of this book.

Not a single day goes by without our benefiting in some significant way from some of the special connections in our networks. Can you make that same claim?

Chapter Two

Test Your Skills:
What Kind and How Skilled of a
Networker Are You?
Assess Your Networking Abilities with
the NQ Pulse Survey

W hat kind of networker are you? Be honest. In this chapter, you will be given the opportunity to take the NQ Pulse Survey to test your networking skills. For now, see if you identify with any of these four types of networking styles:

Askers

Askers are people who proactively keep reaching out to you for resources they need which, for example, might be access to your network or some of your time to advise them. Asker networkers are never bashful about asking but seldom are as proactive offering resources that they have access to that might benefit you. They seldom think of you until they have a need. I also find that the askers seldom even follow back up with a simple thank you. Don't be one of these!

Bill Is a Thoughtless Asker

Bill, a person I met once briefly, heads a major trade association he has been with for about twenty-five years. When we met for lunch recently at his request, he mentioned he was planning on retiring from his full-time role at the end of the year.

Being methodical and wanting to be always prepared, he reached out to me requesting names of employment law attorneys able to work with him to negotiate his retirement package and possibly an ongoing consulting role with the association including helping his successor during the transition.

In cases like this, I always think it best to suggest multiple resources that I think can meet the need. So I contacted partners in three law firms with robust employment law practices asking if they would like to be connected with my friend as a possible new client. I told them all that I would be giving the association leader three firms with which to talk. Hopefully, he would decide to work with one of them.

All three said yes, of course, and thanked me for thinking of them. I connected Bill separately with all three firms via e-mail. The three attorneys all immediately cc'd me on their follow-up with Bill and thanked me again for the connection.

I never heard from Bill again, not even a simple thank you. I don't know if he ever spoke with the three connections and do not know if he decided to move ahead with any one of them. I assume he did nothing with any of the connections I provided.

Interestingly enough, none of the three lawyers I had recommended ever got back to me with the results of their connections with Bill.

Bill, in my mind, will always be an asker. I am not going out of my way ever again to connect him with others in my network for any purpose. Maybe the worst part of this little example is that I paid for the lunch with Bill. He never offered to pick up or split the tab.

When I run into a consistent asker networker, I find myself holding back offering help that I am being asked for and resenting the pressure being applied to provide the help. I certainly don't mind helping people who come to me asking for help. But if it becomes a consistent pattern, then that can get to be old quickly.

If you want to be a successful networker, don't be a regular asker. They wear out their welcome eventually. Don't turn off your connections by approaching networking this way.

Takers

Takers are just what the tag implies. They may not ask you for access to your resources, but if you volunteer resources that you think they will benefit from and enjoy, they will certainly take advantage of your thinking of them. But like the askers, they generally will not reciprocate with suggestions of connecting you with their resources that might benefit you.

Takers can continue to accept your referred resources for a long time without ever thinking of giving back, or even saying thanks. They just don't get it.

This type of networking relationship can last a long time depending on your relationship with the person, the value you place on the relationship, and how much help you want to provide in an effort to have the person succeed or simply like you.

But don't expect much in return from either the askers or the takers.

Traders

Traders are networkers who almost feel compelled to return the favor when you reach out to provide them a resource. Or, if they reach out to you with a suggested resource of their own, they generally will be looking for you to respond similarly. The traders mentally keep score and tend to be willing to keep giving as long as you are returning the favors.

Trader networkers can be successful in developing relationships, but I just believe they would be much more successful if they simply rolled over into the final category of networkers, the givers.

Givers

Givers, in the long run, are the most successful networkers who, if they live long enough, almost certainly will be rewarded big-time from their networking efforts. Givers just commit themselves to being a powerful giver, always on the alert to provide those they value in their network with access to their best resources whether it's a new restaurant suggestion, a good book to read, a great weekend get-away spot, a possible new career opportunity, a potential new customer, or a possible new strategic business alliance.

Committed givers actually do get a lot in immediate returns. They get the good feelings that come from helping others. They cement their relationship even further with people benefiting from their connecting efforts. Word somehow gets around. By generously sharing their resources, they are adding to their personal brand as a reliable resource and someone with a genuine love of helping others.

In the overall scheme of things, the biggest payback you will ever get from committing to improving your networking skills will come when you simply become a giver. Stop worrying and thinking about what you will get back from your time and effort investment in networking and learn to enjoy your own efforts in helping others succeed and reach their potential. Don't try to keep score!

Mickey Was a Giver

Recently I received an e-mail from Brian, a friend commenting on the passing of the founder of the company with which he works. His message sums up a giver:

The funeral on Friday was more of a celebration than anything else…for a life well lived to its fullest.

He was tough but fair…the football coach who wasn't the easiest to play for all the time, but you knew you were a better player because of him.

Here is the short version of my eulogy which asked the question: "How did this humble guy [Mickey from Newark] become so extraordinary when he told everyone how ordinary he was every chance he got?

(1) He outworked everyone
(2) He had insatiable curiosity
(3) He surrounded himself with people smarter than himself all the time
(4) He constantly thought, "What can I do for the other person," way before (if ever) thinking about what they could do for him…and he just saved lives (literally and figuratively) every chance he got
I'm heartbroken but I feel totally blessed to be the "guy he chose" as his right hand/protégé. How lucky was I?

Here's a tip for givers: I spend part of every day linking people with others in my network. E-mail is an efficient tool for doing this. It doesn't take any real time. Maybe ten to fifteen minutes a day spent this way will pay off in spades. Here's a simple example. It took about a minute to generate.

Jay is the COO of a profitable $25-million manufacturing and service company. Scott is the former CFO of a specialty, international publishing company who lost his position when the organization combined European and American operations under one management team. They did not need two well-compensated CFOs battling over the new structure. Here's how I connected them via my e-mail to both:

Jay and Scott:

I think it is worth you two having coffee one a.m.

Jay: Scott is in transition and capable. In the short run he is consulting with a good friend who has distribution and logistics issues in her company. Maybe he can pick your brain for a few minutes? He previously held the top financial position with a major publisher ($200 million in revenues). He knows his stuff internationally.

Scott: Jay is a high-level HR and Senior Counsel Executive with a NJ based, successful distribution/logistics company. He has been with them for several years and has a strong background including in media beyond the current role.

Good luck guys. Holler if I can be helpful in developing your relationship.

One last piece of advice. No matter what type of networker

you are, whenever you ask someone to meet with you over coffee or meal, pick up the tab! When you are invited to meet and expenses will be involved, at least offer to split the bill.

Take the NQ Pulse Survey

In the Bluestone+Killion networking coaching partnership I cofounded in 2012, my partner and I developed our proprietary NQ Pulse Survey that we use to assess a person's networking skills and aptitude. If you would like to have fun and see where you stand, on page 59 is a copy of the NQ Pulse. You also have the option to take it online at www.networkallthetime.com. We will analyze your answers and provide you feedback.

We have found the NQ Pulse Survey to be a realistic assessment of the networking aptitude and skills of thousands of our coaching clients who have taken the survey both before and after we have been coaching them.

Typically we see a fifty to sixty percent improvement in NQ Pulse results following our coaching. And the improvement in skills sticks. Despite what many believe, networking can be learned and will become an important and permanent life and career enhancing skill. Most of our coaching practice serves corporate leaders and professionals with accounting, law and wealth management firms, banks, insurance providers, corporations, charities, and universities. At the outset of our coaching, NQ Pulse scores typically are in the mid-30s on a scale that goes up to 72.

How Good a Networker Are You?

Networking is critical to both the professional and the personal aspects of your life. But many do not possess the skills to use their networks effectively. Do you have the skills to expand your network?

Can you identify opportunities to drive deeper relationships in your current networks? Do you have the networking skills to generate additional revenue for your organization? Are you enriching your life and the lives of those you love through effective networking?

Take the proprietary Bluestone+Killion NQ Pulse. Mark the appropriate boxes. Understanding your NQ Pulse could be one of the more important things you learn about yourself.

Bluestone + Killion
Harnessing the Power of Networking

How Good of a Networker Are You?

Networking is critical to both the professional and the personal aspects of your life. But many do not possess the skills to use their network(s) effectively. Do you have the skills to expand your network? Can you identify opportunities to drive deeper relationships in your current networks? Do you have the networking skills to enhance your life, accelerate your career and generate additional opportunities and revenues for your organization?

Take the Bluestone+Killion NQ Pulse. Mark the appropriate boxes and return the completed Pulse survey to jack@bluestonekillion.com. The results are confidential. Understanding your NQ Pulse could be one of the more important things you learn about yourself!

Your information:

First Name: _____ Last Name: _____

Email: _____

Organization (optional) _____:

Your Personal NQ Pulse:

1. How many total people are in your personal life, social and work related networks?

    [ ] Less than 100 [ ] 100-200 [ ] 200-500 [ ] More than 500

2. To what extent do you actively work on building your network relationships?

    [ ] Never   [ ] Sometimes [ ] Often   [ ] Always

3. To what extent is the relationship with your network members reciprocal? Do you provide substantially more referrals than you receive?

    [ ] Not at all   [ ] Sometimes [ ] Often   [ ] All the time

4. In the past 12 months how many industry conferences, local networking events, networking groups or seminars have you attended?

    [ ] None   [ ] 1-5   [ ] 6-11   [ ] 12 or more

5. How likely are you to bring and expect to use business cards when you go to a "personal" or social type of event where there are likely to be many people you don't know, like a….. wedding, Bar or Bat Mitzvah, funeral or memorial service, important wedding anniversary or birthday celebration ?

    [ ] Never. I like to keep my business and social networking separate
    [ ] Not usually. I don't often mix business and pleasure
    [ ] Usually. Depends on the type of event
    [ ] Always. I never leave home without a stack

6. When you make a new relevant connection, do you schedule a follow up visit or phone conversation within two weeks?

    [ ] No   [ ] Rarely   [ ] Usually   [ ] Yes, definitely

7. Do you find ways to link various members of your networks with each other?

    [ ] Never   [ ] Rarely   [ ] Often   [ ] All of the time

8. Do you regularly set business goals that include developing new business relationships?

    [ ] No   [ ] Rarely   [ ] Often   [ ] All of the time

9. Do you maintain a contact database where you gather information about everyone you meet?

    [ ] No
    [ ] Not really, my contact database is disorganized with scraps of paper, online emails, scattered business cards, contacts in cell phones
    [ ] Basically, but I could do a better job of keeping it current
    [ ] Yes, I have a solid and organized database that is constantly updated

10. Do you work hard to build strong networking relationships internally in your organization, not just with those outside of your company?

    [ ] No   [ ] Rarely   [ ] Often   [ ] All of the time

11. Do you make networking and developing personal connections part of your daily routine?

   [ ] No   [ ] Rarely   [ ] Often   [ ] All the time

12. How important do you think skilled networking should be to both your professional and personal (including) family life?

   [ ] Not really very important to me either in my professional or personal life.
   [ ] Much more important to my personal life. My career is pretty well established.
   [ ] Really important to my professional life and of little benefit to my personal life
   [ ] Extremely important for both my professional and personal life

13. How often in the past month (30 days) have you connected people in your network (by phone, email or in person) who do not know each other and whom you believe should know each other and find ways to do good things together?

   [ ] Not at all
   [ ] Once or maybe twice
   [ ] 3 to 5 times
   [ ] More than 5 times

14. Are there things that stop you from being a strong, pro-active networker such as your personal qualities (shy, quiet, reluctant to reach out to others), you lack the time, you don't really know how to do it effectively, or you lack the necessary training and coaching.

   [ ] Lots of things limit my ability to be a really strong networker
   [ ] I try to network from time to time but don't really get many benefits from the effort
   [ ] I try hard to network effectively. I put time and money into it but wish I could be better.
   [ ] I am a networking powerhouse, way above average, and work at it all the time.

15. Do you believe you have someone in your network that could link you to your top business prospects?

   [ ] No   [ ] Not really   [ ] Sure   [ ] Absolutely

16. When someone does a favor for you, do you send a thank you note or other token of appreciation?

   [ ] No   [ ] Rarely   [ ] Often   [ ] All the time

17. How many groups do you belong to and participate in actively that are focused on networking and new client development?

[ ] None   [ ] One   [ ] Two   [ ] Three or more

18. Do you actively use online social media, like Linkedin, for networking?

[ ] Never   [ ] Rarely   [ ] Often, i.e. weekly   [ ] Always, i.e. daily

19. At work do you or would you feel comfortable submitting expenses to be reimbursed for networking activities?

[ ] No   [ ] Rarely   [ ] Often   [ ] Always

20. How many social groups that may lead to effective personal and professional networking and client development results, such as country clubs, alumni groups, chambers of commerce, rotary and others, do you belong to?

[ ] None   [ ] One   [ ] Two   [ ] Three or more

21. Do you think that participating in a coaching & training program designed to improve your networking and client/business development skills would benefit you professionally and increase the P&L impact you have on your organization?

[ ] Not sure.   [ ] Probably   [ ] Very likely   [ ] For sure. I would really benefit.

22. Do you have an excellent elevator statement or signature story that introduces you quickly and clearly?

[ ] A what?
[ ] I know what that means but don't have one
[ ] I'm still working on it
[ ] Of course, do you want to hear it?

23. Do you believe networking should be taught as a core subject in our school system?

[ ] Not necessarily. There are a lot more important topics to be taught
[ ] Yes at the college level
[ ] Yes both in college and high school
[ ] Yes starting in grammar school and continuing through high school and college

24. At least once a quarter do you reach out to contacts in your network that you haven't been in touch with?

[ ] Never   [ ] Rarely   [ ] More like every 6 months   [ ] Yes

When you complete the NQ Pulse Survey, you will learn that if you score in these ranges you have these networking skills:

60–72– Already have strong networking skills
50–59– Have above average networking skills with room to improve
40–49– Are just slightly above average with your networking skills
30–39– Have half the NQ Pulse you need
Below 30– Have little networking skill and are likely missing a lot in life and in your career

In all cases you can always improve your networking and relationship development skills.

If you take the NQ Survey after reading the book, I expect your score will jump significantly.

Note: The NQ Pulse is the exclusive property of Bluestone+Killion and may not be reproduced without express written permission of the company.

Chapter Three

How to Overcome
Hurdles to Effective Networking

Because I was a slow starter when it came to networking, I have an understanding of the many reasons why the majority of people put so little effort into honing their networking skills and developing important mutually beneficial relationships and, therefore, why they get so little benefit from the process.

Here are the highest hurdles when it comes time to network and grow relationships successfully. Maybe you'll recognize your own challenges and surmount them.

Don't Have a Passion for or
a Commitment to Do It

Being a successful networker starts with believing in the power of it, having a real passion for connecting with people, and being willing to put in the time and energy to become skilled at it. Like anything else, a lukewarm effort won't cut it.

Don't Have Time

This is often cited by both men and women with women feeling they are particularly under the gun time-wise juggling a career, a family, and keeping up the house. While in these tough economic times, when we are all running hard to just stand in place, networking still can be incorporated into your daily life so that disruptions in your schedule are limited.

It's not always easy, but it is possible to make networking strides with minimal interference with the rest of your life. Consider these examples.

• Just talking with more people you meet randomly will yield unexpected benefits without changing any other part of your day (in lines, on the subway, at the gas station, in stores and other places you normally go anyway).

• Have networking meetings over eggs in the morning. You are going to take time to eat so why not do it along with meeting somebody else.

• Concentrate on networking and developing relationships with the groups of people you spend time with nevertheless as part of your normal routine—for example, your neighbors, your club members, or those attending the same house of worship.

One last point about lacking time to network: networking may actually help you free up time that you would otherwise spend researching, looking up things, doing your homework. The more robust your network of valuable relationships, the more easily accessible are the important sources of information you have. Think about it.

Don't Like Selling

While skilled networking in business circumstances certainly will lead to new clients and new sales, I never view networking as "selling." It goes way beyond trying to find and land another client or another deal. Networking to me means learning about other people, sharing with other people, helping other people, building trust with other people, enjoying other people. It's all about building long-term win-win relationships (where you both benefit) based on trust, friendship, integrity, and likeability.

Brian Networks without Even Mentioning What He Does

I had breakfast recently with Brian, a friend and high-powered investment advisor with Neuberger Berman, a major Wall Street firm. He is always on the hunt for new clients with high net worth. Yet when we talked about his approach to networking, he indicated that, unless asked, he never volunteers what he does for a living.

He prefers spending his time with new people learning about them. He clearly devotes energy to networking, and he sells by deliberately not selling.

Don't Know How

This hurdle is legitimate but only up to a point. If you really don't think you know how, then take responsibility for learning how. In this digital age, it is certainly easy to go to Google or YouTube and search for relevant information. This book will turn up on those sites in the future!

Check out local networking groups such as BNI, Rotary, or LeTip International in your area or in your industry and get involved. You have friends and people you work with whom you think do understand networking. Ask them to teach you how.

I was stunned recently when a good friend and fellow graduate from the MIT Sloan School of Business, whom I am guessing annually earns $300,000 to $400,000 or more a year, called and asked if I would teach him to network. He was envious listening to my successful networking experiences and realized what he was missing both professionally and personally. We started spending some breakfast times together, and the progress he made quickly was astounding once he understood the importance and made the commitment to excel.

Don't See the Point and Don't Like Doing It

In other words, they don't understand what life is all about. That it is a two-way street with all of us able to benefit primarily by giving.

Even Business Owners Need Coaching

An early partner in launching one of my new ventures is an example of someone who didn't get the value and importance of networking.

He was in his early forties and a graduate of a major, highly regarded university. He had been an officer in the military. He worked for several years with one of America's leading corporations, when it was still a force to be reckoned with. He previously started and owned his own small chain of boutique stores.

He was tall, fit, well dressed, well groomed, good-looking, and talked with real authority on almost any topic from managing finances to military history to politics to what's wrong with the country. He looked like the total package and should have been a great networker. But he wasn't.

One morning I had him meet a lawyer friend of mine. Later that day my friend called to tell me what a disappointing meeting he had with my partner. His conclusion: "He just doesn't like people and doesn't see the benefit of spending time with people."

That was a real wake-up call for me and made me realize why my partner just wasn't having the impact on the partnership that we both expected. He just didn't see the point of consistently reaching out and meeting people.

The partnership ended within a year of that meeting. I continued running the business successfully for years after he left.

Don't Know With Whom to Network

This is a silly excuse. You should "network" to some extent with everyone you meet. This is very much about reaching out to people, almost all people, and seeing where the connections lead.

The more time you spend talking effectively with people, the better you will get at it. The more you will enjoy it and the more important results you will realize from it. Your personal confidence will soar.

Obviously, though, to benefit the most, you must concentrate your networking efforts on people positioned to be resources for you—that is, target your networking.

Don't Know What to Talk About
When Meeting New People

I hear this often. As a starter, when you meet new people, focus on getting them talking about themselves. Learn as much as you can about them as quickly as you can. You can accomplish this without appearing to "grill" the other person (something our son often kids me about!).

It's the old 80/20 or maybe, in this case, the old 90/10 rule. Spend eighty or ninety percent of the conversation asking a few good questions and then listening carefully instead of talking. Learn to keep asking questions, digging deeper into the other person in a nice, friendly, positive, nonthreatening way. It works. Try it. People love to talk about themselves. Give them the opportunity to talk ninety percent of the time.

I equate this "discovery process" to rock climbing. In both sports you are looking to get a grip so you can take the next step. Once you find the connection points with new people you meet, you are off to the races with ideas for adding value to the other person's life.

Shy and Introverted

Lots of people confess to being this way. I find all of us are a bit inhibited when it comes to networking and meeting new people. I know that is true personally, which many people find hard to believe.

My only advice to you, if this is your personality, is to get over it. The world and life are moving fast. If you elect to stand on the sideline reluctant to reach out to others because you are shy, nobody is going to care. You will miss out on many of the good parts of life. Suck it up. Start talking with people. Overcome your shyness. If necessary go get some professional help that will enable you to open up to others. Or think about joining a group like Toastmasters or take a Dale Carnegie course where you will be forced to come out of your shell. Maybe even taking dancing lessons at a nearby studio would be a good way for you to become more comfortable around people.

If you are not prepared to deal with these issues, then no sense reading further. The rest of the book won't help you much.

When you first make a commitment to being better at networking and relationship development and start to do it, you will start seeing results. Your confidence will zoom. You will feel much better about yourself. The networking process will help bring you out of your shell.

Don't Like Reaching Out Cold to People

It shouldn't come as a surprise that most people, even big-time successful people, often feel uncomfortable cold calling. I certainly still feel that way. But sometimes, if you truly want to meet someone with whom you have no connections, you just have to reach him or her with a call, an e-mail, a LinkedIn message, or maybe an old-fashioned letter.

The worst that can happen is that you never get a response. But how bad can that be? The sun will still come up tomorrow, and you either take another shot at getting through or you take a pass and move on to other people with whom you also want to develop a relationship.

A later chapter deals more with cold calling. Suffice to say, social media can facilitate making "cold" connections.

Cold Calling the Owner of an NBA Franchise

A few years ago our son, Jonathan, the Georgetown University graduate with a degree in finance and accounting and a passion for Hoya basketball, was sent to Memphis by Deloitte, his employer at the time, to work on the year-end audit of a major pharma company. The city had the

Grizzlies, an NBA basketball team headed by Michael Heisley, another Georgetown graduate.

Jonathan sent a letter cold to Michael indicating that, since they were both Hoya graduates and basketball fans, it would be good if they could have dinner one night in Memphis, maybe before one of the Grizzlies' games.

It took a couple of weeks for Jonathan to hear back, but he did get a note indicating it would be fine to meet over dinner when it worked for both of their schedules. He also gave Jonathan the name of his assistant and told him to call her whenever he was in town and wanted tickets to see a game.

Simply reaching out cold to someone with a shared interest led to a positive new relationship.

Sometimes, if you want to meet somebody badly enough and there is no other way to make the connection, you just have to take a deep breath and reach out cold.

Simply Oblivious

I know many people who just don't get what is happening all around them. They never spot opportunities, have limited interests, are not motivated to go particularly far in any aspect of their life, and are basically punching the clock Monday through Friday, just getting by.

Bob K. Might Have Missed a Life-Changing Opportunity

Many years ago I took over ownership and management of Killion Extruders, a failing family-owned industrial equipment manufacturing company, when my dad passed. At the time I was heading two successful consumer magazines that would still require extensive blocks of my time. I needed to groom a backup in the manufacturing company to be my eyes, ears, and voice when I could not be there.

It was a small company without many candidates, but I thought there was one young man Bob K. (under thirty) who, although lacking a college education, had many of the characteristics I was looking for. He worked well with his hands. I am a klutz! He had innate intelligence. (At least I thought so at the time.) He was dependable, had a family with young kids to feed, understood the nature of the business, and got along well with the rest of the internal team and with customers.

I called him into the office one day and explained that I needed to have a first lieutenant, a deputy "me" when I couldn't be around. I offered to put in the time to develop him if he agreed he was a fit and wanted to expand his role and increase his upside, whether he stayed with us or moved on later. He never hesitated in turning me down flat, no hesitation.

"Jack, I love working here and appreciate my job and your suggestion, but I do not want to be like you with all the pressures and all the energy and time you spend trying to save and build the company. I would rather just come in at seven-thirty and leave by four and get home to have dinner with my wife and kids."

I am not certain what his wife would have said if she knew about our conversation, but I guess that never happened. He stayed with the company for another ten years working as a machinist until I sold it to a public UK company. I don't know what happened to him after that. To me he was oblivious to a major opportunity to earn much more and to grow professionally and personally, but who knows?

Arrogance

I see this particularly among some C-level corporate executives and partners in professional law, accounting, financial planning and investment advisory, and other service firms. Somehow many of these people got to their lofty positions through a whole combination of factors: luck, having the right pedigree, having the right education, having the right mentor within the organization, working with a major vital client or customer, or simply riding the crest of a strong economy for years.

The point is they got to where they are without working hard to network and develop strong personal and business relationships. At this stage of their life, they see no need to start working at these activities now.

All of this is fine as a personal lifestyle choice, but it does hurt their organization in a couple of significant ways. It means many of the C-level executives or partners are not leveraging all of their talents to drive the profitable growth of the business, and they are setting a poor example for the next rung of managers and more junior professional staff members who need mentors to help show them the way to win-win networking, relationships and new business development.

Don't Think Networking Can Be Learned

Some believe people either are good or not good at it. We sometimes run into this line of flawed thinking when we (at Bluestone+Killion) are trying to land a coaching engagement in a corporation or professional firm. It's tough to change the opinion of people with this rigid thinking, which is so obviously wrong.

None of us are born as great networkers with real skills for developing successful relationships. We all learn to do these things to varying extents depending on our individual circumstances.

Of course these skills can be developed to a much greater extent by all of us—no exceptions to that statement. I recently learned of STRIVE, an organization committed to helping ex-prisoners get back on their feet. In most cases I doubt the majority of them would have wound up in prison if they had started years earlier developing a high-potential network of quality people. However, I don't think it is ever too late to start working on these skills.

I volunteered recently to start going to STRIVE meetings to talk with the participants about the things they need to do to start developing a quality network that can lead them to a much better life. I have a gut feel this will be a successful and a worthwhile use of my time and their time.

Education as an Issue

We all value education and are careful with our choices. Most parents aim to get their kids into good preschool, elementary, and high schools. They focus on getting them into good colleges to help them develop and enjoy a successful career and enriched life. We think we are being taught the things that will be most important to us, and much of what we learn is of real value. However, much of our education, unfortunately, is of little value.

What is almost never taught is the whole concept of networking and developing exceptionally strong personal and professional relationships. Students are never taught to understand the importance of these skills or how to develop and use them as a real resource for enriching every aspect of their lives.

By the time most get out in the workforce, they are clueless and largely left to figure out the value of skilled networking on their own. Most never do.

I run into unemployed or underemployed recent college graduates floundering badly to find a solid career launch pad. Most tell me that at college they were told by their career counselors, "You have to network to find a good job." Unfortunately they were never told the "how to" of networking.

Don't Like Going to Events or Joining Groups

We all go to events and belong to groups. We just may not realize how much we are "groupies." Birthday parties, anniversaries, reunions, weddings, bar and bat mitzvahs, funerals, and graduations are all events. We join groups when we belong to a golf club, join Rotary or Zonta, play for our company's softball team. And, of course, we become a member of a group the very day we are born because our first group is our family.

So the issue isn't going to events or joining groups. It is more about professional groups and professional events giving us angst, which we deal with in a later chapter.

The Surrounding Culture
Not Supportive of Networking

The cultures in which we live and work can have enormous impact on the quality and results of our networking efforts.

I get more into the importance of personal and business cultures in another chapter, but here recognize that family circumstances—the culture at home—can directly impact the effort and success of our networking.

In our networking coaching programs, we have seen time and time again where the culture of the business organization not only fails to encourage and support effective networking, it also can actually limit networking efforts by people well positioned to network successfully for the benefit of the organization and for themselves. The culture blunts their networking interest and efforts.

Culture of a Major Firm Stops Effective Networking

Our coaching firm was retained by a regional, 150-person CPA firm to train their senior accountants to network more effectively as a way to drive business growth.

We had completed three of the four three-hour workshops we had been brought in to conduct. Obviously the firm had made a significant investment in our fees as well as in the lost billing hours that their staff gave up sitting through our sessions.

We had been covering important points throughout the program and getting good written feedback from participants following each workshop. On a scale of 1 to 5, our overall rating for the first three workshops was a 4.8. Pretty good, we thought.

At the end of the third workshop, one of the more senior accountants in the twenty-five person group receiving our training came up to me, thanked us for our good work, and said it would not have any impact on him and probably not on many of the others. He explained he was already working an average of sixty to seventy hours a week, and he knew that if he brought in additional clients, he would be expected to absorb the new work as well, just adding to the excessive time he already spent working. To make matters worse, his compensation would not change either for landing a new account or for handling it.

We appreciated his honesty. Clearly the culture of the organization was actually acting as a deterrent to encouraging capable professionals from working hard to attract new, profitable clients. There was a breakdown in the firm's business model.

Finally, one excuse most of us can use for not networking effectively is to blame our parents—that is, generally our moms. I am sure your mom warned you not to talk to strangers, which is exactly the opposite of the advice I am giving you here. But sometimes old habits are tough to break.

Being excellent at networking and developing important results-producing relationships is certainly not easy, which is why most people are only marginal at it. We all have some challenges limiting our abilities including our own personal characteristics, the cultures we live in both at home and professionally, or our lack of "how-to" knowledge.

A useful exercise to consider is to list the specific hurdles you face when trying to sharpen these skills and then add a few bullet points next to each, listing the possible steps you can take to eliminate each hurdle.

Chapter Four

The Power of the Business Card and Other Networking Secrets

This book isn't dealing with finding a cure for cancer or landing a man or woman on Mars or solving America's or the world's most critical problems.

I am not a rocket scientist. I never wanted to be and never will be one. What I am sharing with you are simply the basic networking and relationship development observations, experiences, and skills I developed over many decades. They work and have totally enriched every aspect of my life. They have turned up massive personal and business opportunities for me and my family. They can do the same for you.

The book isn't complicated. You will understand everything I write about. You will agree with most of it. You will think some of it is so basic that you already knew it. You may say, "What's the big deal?"

The trick or challenge for you is to take the commonsense suggestions in this book and turn them into your own personal habit-forming actions. Do you do most of the activities suggested in these pages?

If you really put many or most of these thoughts and

recommendations into action every day, then your life will be enhanced, every aspect of it including your professional, your personal, and your family's lives

In their general order of importance, here are keys to being a strong networker and developer of solid relationships that lead to major potential opportunities that can be converted into substantial career developments, profitable business growth, and personal enhancements.

Have the Right Mindset and Be Likeable

If you think you will enjoy and benefit from networking, then I am sure you will. Anyone with a genuinely positive attitude and sincere interest in people can flourish networking. These are the people who can almost always see the bright side of things. Others, whose first reaction to anything new is generally negative, can struggle to do well as networkers. What is your mindset?

Be likeable. People want to be around, spend time with, and help people they like. Likeability is a huge competitive edge when it comes to successful networking. I cannot tell you how to be likeable. I can just emphasize how important it is and how much of an impact it will have on your ability to build exceptional relationships that help shape every aspect of your personal and professional life. We all have our own unique styles and mannerisms when it comes to how we relate to others. Are you likeable?

Make a Commitment to Networking

Networking takes time, energy, and some money, all of which you have to be willing to invest if you are to benefit from pursuing this as part of your daily lifestyle. I have already mentioned a few ways to minimize the disruptions in your life so that you handle all of your other priorities while building up a substantial network of both personal and business connections.

To benefit from networking, you have to be conscious of looking for opportunities every day. They exist all around you all the time. I have a basic philosophy developed over many, many years of doing lots of things. It is that almost anything worthwhile takes a year on average to develop. I think this applies if you are trying to find a new job or land a new major client or have a new addition in your family or plan a vacation to Europe or start a new business or get your son or daughter into a college that will help them in the future.

If you do not initiate and start to nurture a new contact today, don't expect to harvest the results a year from today.

Be Patient

Networking seldom generates immediate major results. Establishing the right kind of long-term relationships built on friendships, trust, and respect takes time to bear real fruit.

I know that almost anything worth accomplishing takes a year or longer. Be prepared to invest that length of time in any relationship you consider important.

Focus on Helping Others and Don't Worry What You Get in Return

Anyone who is any good at networking at all will tell you one of the real keys (maybe "the key") to excelling at it is to focus on giving and helping other people. I emphasized this earlier.

Networking is not about keeping score and making certain

you get paid back for all the effort you put into helping others. Life isn't that simple or fair. Over the years, if you are a skilled networker and developer of real relationships, you will help many more people than will help you. That's just a fact of life. It only shows that you "get it" more than most people.

Our economy is increasingly dependent on service businesses. We no longer are a global manufacturing power. In a manufacturing economy, people bought products that met their needs. So, in most cases, the product itself was the basis for the relationship between the provider and the customer, such as General Motors and their cars, GE and their home appliances, IBM and their computers.

In a service economy like we have today, many providers are likely to be able to deliver an equal or even a superior service at an equal or lower cost. So the depth of the commitment between the client and the service provider generally comes down to the depth of the personal relationship that develops between the two.

Constantly be looking for ways to contribute to someone else's successful life. Connect them with others in your network, recommend things to them, share your ideas, thinking, and experiences with them. Be a sounding board for their ideas.

Eventually what goes around will come around. Out of the blue somebody totally unexpected will do something nice for you that will affect your life.

In the meantime, as a giver, you will be getting many of these valuable benefits in return:

• Your reputation and value as an important resource to others will go up.

• The strength of your relationships will increase.

• You will get real personal satisfaction making a difference in the lives of others.

- You will be perceived as someone who can add important value and make a difference.

Be a giver and a connector and not an asker, taker, or trader. Throughout the rest of your life, you will meet thousands of givers, traders, askers, and takers. Eventually most of the others, besides the givers, will fall by the wayside as you lose interest in people who do not share your passion for helping and adding value to others.

Talk to Everyone

It's free and can't hurt. Every day you run into many people. Start a conversation with them. This means talking with people in the elevator, riding a bus or subway, standing next to you at one of your kid's ball games, sitting next to you at a Giants or Knicks game, in the checkout line at the food store, in line at Staples, sitting next to you at the next Broadway play you attend, staying at the same B&B, people in the lobby of your building, people in line at your bank. TALK TO EVERYBODY!

Follow Your Passions and Interests

We all live and work in "clusters" of people connected in various ways to the things we are passionate about and interested in. That's where you should concentrate much of your networking and relationship development efforts. These clusters will change at different points in your life as your interests and passions change.

For example, twenty years ago, Judy and I were heavily involved in thoroughbred horse racing. We owned and lived on a farm. We bred, raised, and trained our own race horses. We emerged as leaders in the industry at both the state and national level. We went to the major horse auctions. We read the main industry publications. We went to the Kentucky Derby every year for about twenty years.

So, obviously, we spent a great deal of our networking efforts within this thoroughbred racing cluster and benefited enormously as our connections led us to the best vets and blacksmiths, taught us about the proper way to feed and care for the growing and performing thoroughbred, and uncovered relatively unknown but top-quality breeding stock. Our foundation breeding mare was one we bought unraced off the race track for $1,500 based on a friend's recommendation that we take a look. It turned out she was a half-sister to the great Secretariat who was delivered a few years later by the same mare that was the mom of our amazing good luck $1,500 purchase!

Now our interest in the racing business has waned and has been replaced by other areas of similar passion including launching several of our own businesses and mentoring high school and college kids. So instead of focusing networking efforts on the racing industry, we focus effort on people involved in the financial, entrepreneurial, and training/education worlds.

What are your main interest areas? Are you concentrating your networking efforts there? Your clusters are likely to include people, for example, in these areas:

- Your extended professional internal and external networks

- Your family and your friends

- Your neighborhood

- Your high school and college alumni groups

- The clubs you belong to

- The nonprofits you help support

These groups are all likely to create great personal and professional networking opportunities.

Concentrate on Staying in Touch and Growing Relationships

Let's assume that you live to eighty and on average you meet and talk with ten new people a day. Even the briefest encounter counts in this equation. That means over the course of your lifetime you meet nearly 300,000 people.

Obviously, you cannot develop meaningful relationships with all of them. You have to consistently prune your network so you are concentrating your networking efforts on the people that make the most sense for you at the various times and stages of your life. This comes down to managing your contacts effectively.

Carry Your Business Cards Everywhere, No Exceptions

If you are employed, you likely have business cards. Even if you are not working, you need to get your own business cards. What's the advantage of not having one or ever leaving home without them?

You can never anticipate where or when you might need or want to hand one of your cards to someone you find particularly interesting, important, or relevant. It gives them the tool they need to follow up with you.

Too many people feel that they cannot or should not mix personal and business. I am not sure why. That just doesn't make any sense to me. As a result, these same people often leave their cards home when doing something non–work related. Why? What's the advantage of that?

Heidi and the Lost Opportunity

Heidi, a young friend, did not see the value in handing a business card to an accountant she met for the first time when we were having breakfast recently.

I met for the first time in over a year with Heidi, an exceptional young woman who recently completed her master's degree course work that prepared her to become a family counselor. Now she needed to do some internship type of counseling at a center near her university.

Heidi is bright, passionate about her career, motivated, and under self-imposed pressure to attract clients. Her compensation at the center where she is counseling families is tied directly to the number and quality of personal clients (revenues generated) that she lands.

While Heidi and I were having our eggs, my accountant came over to our booth to say hello. He saw me come into the diner where he had been having breakfast with one of his clients. He joined our conversation for a few minutes. When he left, I asked Heidi why she did not exchange business cards with the accountant whom she just she met for the first time.

Her response blew me away: "Why, I already have an accountant?"

Heidi still isn't experienced enough to know that every new person she meets is a possible referring source of clients for her new career. The accountant has two partners, and I assume at least five hundred clients for his firm. Given America's fifty percent divorce rate, some of his clients must have personal and family issues. I doubt Joe, the accountant, knows many or any professionals with appropriate family counseling skills to whom he might refer clients needing guidance. She could have been a good resource for the accountant to access when working to add *value, besides doing good accounting work, to his clients.*

Since Heidi did not exchange cards, she lacks the ability to follow up, telling him how much she enjoyed meeting him and summarizing the types of new clients she is looking for. In a good follow-up like that, it would have been important for her to ask the accountant to summarize the types of new clients he is looking for so that she might look for ways to add value to his work by making appropriate referrals.

This random meeting could have been the start of a significant business relationship between them. We will never know.

I take my cards with me everywhere—every business meeting (duh!), neighborhood cookouts, weddings, bar and bat mitzvahs, birthday and anniversary celebrations and even funerals. In fact, because I am involved in several different businesses, I usually take a collection of my various cards with me from my different ventures so that I can hand over the one that makes most sense for each conversation.

Networking at a Funeral

Some people when they hear me suggest that funerals can create good networking opportunities look at me a little cross-eyed.

Steve, a friend of over forty years, passed away recently from heart disease. Besides being a friend, he was also the lawyer for us when we started Country Music magazine. My wife and I drove up to Connecticut for the service in Steve's temple. After the service, everyone (over a hundred of us) was invited back to his son's home in Westport to have some lunch and reminisce.

The atmosphere in the temple was somber and sad. Everyone had their own private thoughts and memories of Steve, the common friend we had lost. Tears flowed including mine. But later, back at the son's magnificent home, the mood turned distinctly positive as we all started to share stories about our times with Steve.

The majority of people there I had never met including his roommates from Vanderbilt law school from forty-five years ago, high school friends with whom he had stayed in touch, clients of his law practice, partners in various firms he worked with, his sons and daughters and grandchildren.

It was sad and almost magical at the same time. We were all there to celebrate a special friend. Thankfully I happened to wear a jacket that had a big handful of my business cards in a pocket from when I attended some other event. I went through almost all of my cards, as many of Steve's friends wanted to stay in touch after our initial conversations.

I relearned a valuable lesson that day. Always bring my cards with me. Make it easy for people to follow up and stay in touch.

Networking with a Drummer at a Memorial Service

Bob Z, the founder of an enormously successful hedge fund in which my Eagle Rock Diversified Fund is invested, passed recently. We were invited to the memorial service at the Botanical Gardens in the Bronx. About four hundred attended.

Following the service, we all had a fabulous lunch in one of the magnificent buildings in the gardens. Judy and I loaded our plates at the various carving stations and grabbed a couple of seats at a table of four. Soon after, another couple joined us.

They were obviously successful. They too were investors in the same hedge fund. She was a partner in a long-established Wall Street firm. Her well-dressed husband in an exquisite dark gray suit also looked like he probably had a similar successful career in the financial sector.

As I started asking questions, getting my new friend Sammy to talk so I could find the "finger holds," I learned that Sammy in fact did

*not work on Wall Street. He was a drummer. Now in his fifties, Sammy
had performed with many of the giants in the music industry including
Michael Jackson, Aretha Franklin, Billy Joel, Cindy Lauper, the Beach
Boys, and countless others. He played the drums with Hank Williams Jr.
on Monday Night Football.*

*During our interesting conversation, I learned that Sammy was
drumming on Broadway in the hit show Kinky Boots. A couple of days
later, I bought tickets to see the show and sent Sammy an e-mail telling
him we were coming and would be enjoying his drumming. He quickly
responded with an invitation to join him backstage after the show to be
introduced to the cast members and to learn how a successful Broadway
show operates.*

*The experience, totally unexpected, was a once-in-a-lifetime type
of thing that resulted only because both of us felt comfortable networking
and getting to know each other at a memorial service for a common
friend. I am sure this new friendship will flourish in the future.*

Note: Business cards make great gifts for almost everyone. We bought
our son business cards when he was about thirteen. He certainly didn't
like or appreciate the gift as in, "Kids don't have business cards. I don't
want business cards." But Jonathan was and still is an excellent golfer
who competed while in high school at tournaments up and down the
East Coast as well as in Europe. We often dropped him off at the local
course where the starter would connect him with others willing to
play with a kid. He usually smoked them! At the end of the round of
everyone having an enjoyable time and wanting to play again, Jonathan
lacked a way (other than writing on the back of a scorecard) of letting
people know how to reach him.

Of course we had discussions with Jonathan about how to use
his new business cards and to whom to give them from a personal
safety point of view. We always talked about people he played with and
to whom he gave cards. Obviously parents need to be involved with

their kids' relationships.

At first Jonathan didn't like the title we put on his card—Evangelist—but eventually he realized it was cool when others in his school started asking their parents to get them business or "connection" cards.

As you can imagine, Jonathan has turned into a networking and relationship developing powerhouse. It is a core strength that helps separate him from the herd professionally. The partners heading the turnaround/restructuring firm he works with know that they can bring Jonathan to any event and he will handle himself effectively. They know in his downtime (breakfast, some lunch times, evenings, and some weekends) he is meeting new people and starting to develop relationships that will eventually be assets to his firm in a myriad of ways.

At the other end of the spectrum was my mom for whom I bought "business" cards when she was still alive in her mid-nineties and living in a nursing home. It pumped her up to hand out cards to the staff, other residents, visiting doctors, and families of other residents. She loved the title we gave her—The World's Best Mom.

Recently I met a highly decorated, thirty-nine-year-old lieutenant colonel in the US Army, a West Point graduate with lots of combat experience. He has a little over three years to go before possibly leaving the military. In the meantime, he is gearing up to get his MBA to better position himself for reentering the civilian world.

I asked for his business card and was shocked when he said he didn't have one. Apparently in the military, it is easy to reach others in the service. But he misses the point. He should be developing his civilian network right now so that it is in place when it comes time to launch a new career and he needs access to people and opportunities in the business world. Having a business card to exchange in his case is a must.

Board Members without Relevant Business Cards

I ran into an interesting group of people recently, all lacked a business card they needed, at least in my opinion. I had been invited to spend three hours coaching the high-powered board of a major charity to network more effectively. The CEO of the charity felt the board members could be doing a better job of generating financial support for the cause and creating strategic alliances with their target educational institutions. This charity operates to teach teachers how to teach financial literacy to elementary school and high school kids.

At the beginning of the evening's discussion, I passed around my business cards and asked for theirs. They handed theirs over. Surprisingly, none of the cards identified them as being with the charity. The cards they gave me were from major law firms, accounting firms, banks, and Wall Street organizations. Impressive, but not the tool I think they need when meeting people for the charity's business. I made that point at the meeting and think they subsequently ordered business cards from the charity.

Prior to meeting I checked the board members out on LinkedIn. I always try to do a LinkedIn background check on new people I meet. I hope you do this as well. What I discovered blew me away. None of the board members listed their involvement with the charity on their LinkedIn profile. If they approached you for funding support for the charity and you could not find mention of it on their LinkedIn profile, how important would you think the charity was to them?

Bottom line, it is hard to imagine anyone really who shouldn't have their own "business" cards including grandparents, babysitters, interns, caddies, taxi drivers, stay-at-home moms and dads, and high school and certainly college kids. Think about it. Who can you get cards for?

Here's another important point about business cards. Make them easy to read. Many of us positioned to help others are older and have poor eyesight. Why make it tough or impossible to quickly read your card because the copy is too small or too muted and shaded or in too tricky a script? Keep it simple.

When you get a new card from someone, treat it with respect. Read it when it is handed to you. Find a reason to make a positive comment. Use it to trigger a conversation with the other person: How long have you been with the organization? What does your position involve? What are your biggest challenges? What markets do you serve?

Don't just stick the card immediately in your wallet, purse, or pocket as though it had no importance. Show some respect. This is particularly important when you are out of the country and involved in other cultures.

One last little tip for making your business card more memorable: find something relevant to print on the back side. On the reverse side of the card I use as a partner in our networking coaching firm, I had this printed: "Jack, I learned more from you in 120 minutes than I received from a number of so-called 'experts' in five years! I am not exaggerating!"

Just putting a quote from a client almost always creates a conversation.

Have an Effective Elevator Pitch

I actually hate the word pitch. It reminds me of someone at the carnival hawking some silly thing or a used car salesman. Let's call how you introduce yourself your thirty-second profile—the amount of time you would have on an elevator with someone going up a few floors.

There are books and YouTube videos galore dealing with this

topic. Do some homework. This is important. There is no one best way. You have to figure out how best to position yourself with a crisp and to-the-point introductory profile when you meet new people.

You need to have a clear statement of who you are when you meet people for the first time. Actually, you may need several clear statements depending on which part of your extended network you are in. For example:

• If you are picking your son or daughter up from a friend's house, you may simply be little Billy's mom or dad.

• If you are active in a local nonprofit, you may introduce yourself as Tom, a board member with the Do Good Foundation, which is dedicated to raising the literacy rate among disadvantaged young children in our inner cities.

• You may be a surgeon at a major hospital which means you are Dr. Jones, at the nationally ranked cardiac care center at Big Time Hospital, where you specialize in complex heart operations and replacements that have one of the highest survival rates in the country.

• You may be a partner in the international ABC accounting firm where you specialize in handling complex global tax issues for international corporations.

Developing and honing your profile takes thinking and practice to get it exactly right. Make a game of it. Practice it at home with your family or with friends. Have them develop and practice their own profiles. Do the same thing when you go out for lunch with colleagues at work. Help them sharpen their profiles while they are helping you hone yours.

I recently took a bright, talented summer intern with me to a meeting with a major law firm in the morning and then to a second law firm meeting in the afternoon. The meetings were to develop strategic alliances with Judy's Garden State Woman Education Foundation.

We asked the intern to give her thirty-second profile and business cards to everyone. We made sure she had cards made at Vista Print when she joined us. She had never had cards before. Bad mistake for all college students! Her profile was this:

Hi, I am Dana and I go to Susquehanna University in Pennsylvania where I just finished my sophomore year with a dual major in communication and marketing. I am working with Jack and Judy during the summer in a variety of their companies and projects in which they are involved.

Dana did a good job and people responded positively. At our next meeting, we suggested Dana add a couple of other comments:

I am also helping Jack and Judy learn to use social media more effectively in their work, and I am excited about my upcoming study-abroad semester in Australia. What kind of law do you practice?

Just by adding these two little comments and the ending question, Dana triggered an immediate, much stronger reaction. Other than high school and college kids, most of the rest of us are struggling to know about and use the various social media tools. The lawyers really wanted to engage Dana in a discussion about social media. And it was clear that they all were a bit envious of Dana's upcoming semester studying in Australia. That too triggered a lot of comments and questions. And by simply ending her profile with the question: "What do you do?" she showed her interest in learning about them and made the conversation two ways.

Tweaking her thirty-second profile or elevator speech accomplished the basic goal of encouraging the listeners to want to know and learn more about her. In a small way she started to separate herself from the herd of other young people out there trying to carve out a career for themselves. The second law firm's marketing director quickly e-mailed Dana indicating she would like to treat for a follow-up breakfast or a lunch meeting. Maybe next summer Dana will intern there!

In a recent career development workshop I ran to coach

professionals in a major national professional firm, I asked the twenty participants each to stand up and give their thirty-second profile. What jumped out of the exercise like a sore thumb was how vastly different each one's approach to basically describing the firm itself was. In some cases (only a few), their firm description would have made me want to learn more. In too many cases, the way they described the firm made it seem pedestrian and limited in scope. I would have had zero interest in learning anything else about the firm.

What was clear is that the firm's leaders with over 1,500 professionals in over a dozen offices had never taken even a few minutes to decide and communicate to everyone in the organization exactly how they should position the firm when they meet new people. Seems to me that needs to be corrected immediately for all current employees and should be built into future new-hire orientation sessions.

One point I want you to take away from this book is that networking and relationship development is not and should not be all grim and serious. Lighten up. It should be fun, exciting, interesting for sure, adventurous. It is how you are going to learn what's going on and what's available in the world. We live in a global community. We all can learn from and share with each other.

Make everything about you interesting. To the extent you can, make your business cards interesting and certainly make your thirty-second profile interesting.

At a minimum your profile or elevator speech needs to include:

- Your name

- Your title or some indication of what you do. Particularly young people not yet working should have fun and be creative with their title. A high school student I interviewed recently for MIT handed me his card when we first met. His title was "Dreamer without Borders," which I thought was fantastic.

- Name of your organization (if you are with one)

- Some little nugget of information that sets you apart from all the others in your same circumstances

To emphasize, here's an effective way to end your speech. Remember one of our golden rules, listen eighty to ninety percent of the time. So one technique that works when giving your profile and when it makes sense is to simply end by asking: "And what do you do for a living?" That simple little question demonstrates your interest in them and gets them talking about themselves so that you start to spot opportunities to possibly add value to their careers and lives.

Inject a Little Humor into Your Conversations

It's an important part of being likeable. Life does not always have to be deadly serious. People enjoy smiling and laughing. Give them the opportunity by finding ways to add humor to the discussion. Even making a little fun of yourself can be a good ice breaker. People almost always respond well when I confess to being a dinosaur when it comes to using social media and new technologies. It happens to be true!

Be an Interesting Conversationalist and a Probing Questioner

A simple enough requirement for success, but to me it implies several important subparts of the concept.

You don't have to be a back-slapping life-of-the-party type. In fact, many of the most effective networkers I know are relatively low-key, quiet, unassuming types. If you are quiet versus loud, people really have to pay close attention to what you are saying (as long as what you are saying is interesting and important).

Be genuine in your interest in the person or people with whom you are talking. There are few things worse than being in a conversation with a phony baloney who could care less about you and the things you are talking about. People can usually spot phonies a mile away. Don't be one. And if you happen to be talking to one, then I think you should certainly feel comfortable excusing yourself from the conversation and moving on to meet and talk with others who will find you interesting and worth spending time with talking.

Be inquisitive about the other person or people. Ask questions, dig into the other person's life and their career. If people are comfortable being with you, they will open up and share most or all aspects of their lives. People for the most part like to talk about themselves. Ask interesting, thought-provoking questions. Show real interest. Learn about them. As I said earlier, talk ten to twenty percent of the time and listen the rest of the time.

The ability to consistently ask leading questions without being resented for being aggressive or invasive is clearly a critical skill you need to develop to excel in networking and creating sustainable relationships.

One concept I have is that everyone you meet opens a door to their world. How wide the door opens is up to your ability to develop chemistry with the person. With the right relationship, everything or nearly everything about their world will be available to you including their ideas, experiences, resources, and connections. If you have a thousand relationships in your network, you potentially have access to a thousand different worlds. How mind-blowing is that?

Another concept I have is that every question I ask and every answer I get back is like getting a finger hold climbing a mountain. In every conversation I am looking for ways to add value to the other person. The more finger holds I create, the more likely I am to come up with ways to add value. That's one of the real keys to building successful relationships. Give. Then give some more and then give some more after that. Keep giving.

Be interesting with things to talk about. If you are as dull as a stone who would want to talk with and get to know you? Nobody. Why would they? Your life should be just one long learning curve. Learn something new every day. Like everything worth having in life, being interesting takes effort and time. And it is never too late to start being more interesting. Here are some simple steps you can take to be more interesting:

Read anything, but read. I am so hung up on this that I never will again hire anyone who says they do not read regularly. When I was growing up, there wasn't any TV. Listening to the radio and reading were two ways we filled our time and got information. Today my wife and I start most days by going to the local corner store and buying at least three newspapers along with cups of tea. Normally we go to a local park and read the three papers and have our tea well before seven-thirty or eight in the morning.

Follow your interests and passions. Read about the things that are of most interest to you. Read either in print or online with your Kindle, Nook, or iPad. I am on a kick at the moment trying to read a book a week. Given all the things I am involved with, it's not easy. But I think it is important so I work at it. So should you.

Watch some quality TV. I know this isn't easy with all the "dumbing down of America" programs that are on around the clock. But try to find current and relevant talk shows with interesting guests, hosts, and topics. Morning Joe is one of our favorite talk shows. Try some of the other nontrivial cable stations such as Discovery, National Geographic, the Food and the History channels. Again, follow your interests and passions but, for sure, you should be interested in what is going on around you every day. Watch the news at night. Ever think about watching the BBC news broadcasts?

Listen to quality content radio. We all spend way too much time in the car. Use some of it to listen to some relevant stations, NPR being one. And there are others. Keep station-hopping until you come to something that interests you.

The Power of the Business Card
and Other Networking Secrets

Spend time with smart, energetic, creative, interesting, successful people. Use every opportunity to listen and learn from those around you. For the most part, people are fascinating. Learn from them. Keep asking questions. Have the mindset that you can learn from everybody.

Travel. It is eye-opening. I think everybody should travel as much as possible to as many places as possible as frequently as possible. Money is an issue for most of us. But still, there cannot be many better ways to spend some of the few discretionary dollars we have than on travel. I love to hear about young people traveling abroad with their friends, staying at hostels, riding the railroads, eating different foods in out-of-the-way places, seeing the world. I recommend every college student try to study abroad for at least a semester. It is a life-changing experience.

Our son, Jonathan, while at Georgetown University, studied one semester in Denmark and used the weekends and time out of class to travel throughout Europe, from Russia to Spain and Italy and many of the places in between. He left a college student and came back a young man able to make it on his own in whatever country or city he finds himself.

One final word about how importantly I view using lots of creative ways to continually be learning. For at least past fifteen years, I have interviewed high school seniors applying to MIT. Eventually in every conversation I get around to asking: What do you read? What do you watch on TV? Who do you hang out with? How much traveling have you done alone or with your family? I find it difficult to recommend any young person to as competitive a place as MIT if he or she is not truly interested in learning and expanding, using all the available tools and experiences. I have a high success rate regarding my admissions recommendations.

Keep Notes When Convenient and Possible

We all meet many people during our typical weeks, and it is easy to forget and lose track of some of the key points covered in discussions. I almost always have a simple notebook with me at every meeting I have. Whenever possible, I jot down the key points we are talking about along with the person's name and date of the discussion. These notes are invaluable when I follow up. Plus, note taking demonstrates to the other person that you consider the discussion important enough to keep track in writing.

Smartphones also offer note-taking apps, which I haven't mastered yet, but many people use them for notes.

Follow Up

Always send a thank-you note or e-mail or call the person taking time to meet with you. When growing relationships, simple manners count.

Recently I had breakfast with one person and lunch with another. I knew both. Both had suggested we meet. Both were looking for some career input from me. I treated for both meals. I got a follow-up e-mail that evening from one of the two but have heard nothing from the other, and two weeks has gone by. How do you think I will react the next time he suggests we meet?

Follow up quickly—within twenty-four hours or even less time. If you wait forty-eight hours, the impact of your follow-up is dampened. By then most people will have forgotten much of what you discussed. Longer than forty-eight hours and I think a follow-up is nearly pointless since you have already sent a clear signal that the meeting or conversation you had wasn't a priority for you.

Follow up with whatever information or action step you

promised during your meeting/conversation. Besides including a "thanks for meeting" note, deliver the specific thing(s) you promised. Always under promise and over deliver. Being dependable is certainly one of the keys to being a great networker.

In your follow-up, make a suggestion for the next step you propose taking to continue to develop the relationship.

Follow up any way you feel comfortable with, which can mean e-mail (my favorite most of the time), phone, or by mail. Some use handwritten notes, which they think add a "personal" touch to the follow-up. And, of course, it is usually smart to follow up sometime later on the follow-up.

Add Value in a Relationship. Be a Connector.

I always am looking for ways to connect people in my network whom I believe should know each other and will benefit from having the relationship. E-mail and social media make this easy to do.

People will appreciate you connecting them with other good people when you see a real fit.

I try to spend the first few minutes of each day connecting various people in my network. It's ten or fifteen minutes well spent. It shows my contacts that I value their friendship and capabilities and am totally comfortable introducing them to similarly high-quality people with whom they should be able to develop win-win relationships.

I believe that too many professionals including lawyers, bankers, and accountants pursue the wrong business model believing that they exist to "do transactions." Using this approach to build a book of business to me can be high risk. Clients, for the most part, can always find a competent replacement professional to handle the same transactions less expensively.

I would rather see these same professionals adopt as their basic business model that they are really in their profession to help their clients grow and thrive. That should be their practice development focus. Wake up each morning thinking how can I make my clients' businesses even more successful? What resources and connections do I have that I can share with my clients that potentially will have a positive impact on their businesses and/or careers and lives?

I have been working with accounting and law firms of all sizes for over forty years and seldom have I had one suggest a couple of resources or contacts that they think I should know and that could help drive profitable growth for my businesses. Nevertheless, their invoices show up on schedule.

One word about connecting people, make certain you know both people well enough to know that a new, suggested connection makes sense and is likely to be appreciated. Because my brand includes having a robust network, I am often asked to make potentially important connections by people I barely know. I am highly reluctant to do this until I get to know the person asking for help better. Following is an e-mail I received recently that clearly demonstrates this point:

Dear Mr. Killion,

How are you?

I was one of the students that attended your lecture at Fairleigh Dickinson University a few months ago. When we met, I expressed my interest in attending Georgetown University to pursue a graduate degree in political science. You gladly gave me the e-mail address of your son, Jonathan.

Unfortunately, because I did not take the GRE, I was not able to apply to be admitted for the fall semester. As a result, I have decided to take a year off from school and work to gain experience in a related field. I am currently looking for a job or an internship at any law firm in NJ or NYC. If you know of any, can you let me know? Thank you for always being so helpful.

Note: Even though I barely knew this recent college graduate, I was willing to connect him with my son who went to Georgetown and is president of the Georgetown University Alumni Club in New Jersey. Jonathan is always looking to attract potentially talented people to his alma mater. However, I did not feel comfortable tapping into my network of successful lawyers and suggesting that this student would be a viable employee or intern. I had no idea how effective the student might be working in a law firm. I did not want to hang my credibility with my lawyer connections on someone I barely knew.

A better approach would have been for the student to ask to meet me so we could get to know each other, and then he could outline his career plans with me. I would have been willing to do that.

Have an Objective and a Plan

Have an objective and a plan when you meet someone. Go into every scheduled meeting with at least some goal, which could be as simple as just spending quality time and sharing experiences with an interesting person to whom you have been referred. You will always learn something when meeting new people.

Or your objective can be much more specific. For example, I manage the Eagle Rock Diversified Fund, a fund of hedge funds that I launched in 2001. I am always interested in attracting appropriate investors. If one of my objectives in a meeting is to explain my fund with a goal of getting subsequent introductions to potential investors, I may go with a written summary of my objective for the meeting. When I do this, I always ask the other person to follow up with me with a brief written outline of the types of contacts he or she would like me to introduce to him or her.

Here's a quick version of the type of written request for connections I often use after meeting someone positioned to refer me to relevant new accredited investor contacts.

Referrals I value for my Eagle Rock Diversified Fund

With the goal of growing my Eagle Rock Diversified Fund, with its $250,000 minimum investment requirement, I value being connected to the following types of people:

• *Accredited individual investors looking to diversify their portfolio and open to considering an alternative form of investing—in hedge funds*

• *Decision-makers investing the assets of small to midsize pension funds*

• *Fee-only investment advisors with accredited investors open to considering hedge funds for their portfolios*

• *Professional advisors to accredited individual investors including estate attorneys and accountants*

I will appreciate receiving from you a similar written outline of the potential new and important contacts I might introduce to you.

Very few people, who are otherwise excellent networkers, think to put their meeting objective(s) in writing, which, to me, if done tastefully, can only make the meeting more productive for both sides.

Obviously, when you meet, be positive, upbeat, energetic, friendly, real, natural, and enthusiastic about spending the time together.

I am totally turned off meeting rigid "empty suits" lacking any real creativity, energy, ideas, and passion. I have had lots of meetings over the years with "professionals" in their tailored handmade suits and power ties who were total turnoffs.

For you to be an effective networker and developer of successful, productive relationships, people need to be able to relate to you. I have been in partnerships involving generally capable people whom clients indicated, "I just can't relate to your partner." That's obviously not good.

When you meet people, just be yourself. Be genuine. Be authentic. That will be more than good enough.

I recommend you read The Happiness Advantage by Shawn Acher. It effectively documents the need and benefits from being a happy, positive person. It sounds like motherhood but it is not. How many people do you know who are basically unhappy and miserable?

Actively Reach Out to New People

Successful networking isn't about sitting around waiting for lightning to hit or someone to reach out to you. If there is someone important you want or need to meet, take the initiative in making the first contact suggesting a follow-up phone call or meeting. E-mail and LinkedIn can be appropriate ways to reach out to someone cold for the first time.

Pick Convenient Places and Times for Meetings

Pick convenient places and times to suggest for meetings. Because I am generally a meat-and-potatoes-type of person, I like to keep things simple. I often suggest meeting for the first time for breakfast at a diner midway between us.

Most people can find time for a quick breakfast before the day starts. Certainly this is usually easier, faster, and less expensive than scheduling a lunch or dinner meeting. I seldom arrange a networking type of meeting at night. This is just one of the ways I fit networking into my daily lifestyle. If I do anything work-related at night, it has to be a special opportunity.

Sometimes I also like to suggest late afternoon meetings (say at four or four-thirty) over coffee or tea at a local Starbucks. Most people appreciate and can arrange to get out of work a bit early for a relevant, business-related networking discussion.

Often but not usually, I will arrange the first meeting at the other person's office. This obviously can make it easier for the person I am meeting, and it gives me a better chance to understand their business. The downside of course is that it can be tough to get undivided attention with phones ringing and people coming in and out of the meeting room. So sometimes these meetings happen after normal working hours.

I generally find it much easier to quickly establish rapport if we are meeting out of their office and in a low-key type of place for a coffee, tea, eggs, or lunch.

Specific Thoughts Relative to Women Networking

Through Judy's Garden State Woman Education Foundation, I have coached and trained hundreds of professional, corporate, and business-owning women to network and initiate new two-way positive relationships.

Hundreds of terrific women are in my active database. I stay in touch with many of them, just as I stay in touch with my male contacts. I don't view my contacts as male versus female. I just want to concentrate my networking efforts on quality people with whom I see a real fit.

However, I am surprised that so few women proactively reach out to me suggesting we meet or talk or to provide a valid new connection or to ask for my help or provide their help in some way. The general lack of reaching out to men among women, based on my personal experience, astounds me.

The Power of the Business Card
and Other Networking Secrets

Almost without exception the issue always comes up: "How do I reach out to a man without him thinking I am 'hitting' on him?" I believe most men are not thinking like this. Most of us just want to keep moving ahead, working effectively with as many relevant, quality people as possible, whether men or women.

All of us are under enormous pressures these days to deal with all of the issues challenging us as a country and individually. I doubt many of us are looking to complicate our lives by working to develop extraneous relationships for the wrong reasons.

Ladies, I think you can give us (or at least the vast majority of us) more credit than that.

You can make it crystal clear you are absolutely reaching out for legitimate business reasons by suggesting you meet in their or your office during normal work hours, at a diner for morning eggs or at a coffee shop for a late-day tea or coffee or as your guest at some business function or agree to meet at a relevant event or in a group in which you are both participating.

If you remain uncomfortable reaching out to men with whom you see valid opportunities to build a successful business relationship, you are shutting yourself off from fifty percent of the people possibly positioned to enhance your career and your life. That doesn't seem like such a smart idea to me.

Keep Track of the People You Meet

Too many of us are proficient at collecting business cards but not so good organizing them effectively. I bet most readers of this book can look with frustration at a stack of business cards sitting on their desk not knowing what to do with them.

This book isn't about data management, so all I am going to do is to emphasize the importance of keeping track and prioritizing your contacts and developing and maintaining a database with them.

Constant Contact is one workable and efficient system if you are planning to stay in touch with your people using e-marketing. Mail Chimp is another contact management system some people prefer.

Think about whether it makes sense to get a scanner to run the business cards through. They are not expensive with many models on the market to choose from.

When prioritizing the people you meet, consider the same approach I use in tracking and sorting my new contacts into four categories.

I meet terrifically interesting people for the first time almost every day, sometimes making fifty or more new connections a month. I need a simple way to just track who they are. So every month, I develop an Excel spreadsheet that carries a daily running list of contacts I want to make certain I remember and possibly work with in some way in the future.

I assign priorities, as follows, to the new people I meet and estimate that only twenty-five percent have a high priority rating in my mind. These are the new connections I need to nourish and grow.

Contacts				
Date				
First Name				
Last Name				
Organization				
E-mail				
Phone				
Priority (1 - 4)				

Priority 4: Chuck it. If you see no foreseeable reason to keep this card or try to build a relationship with the person, stick the card in a box in case things change in the future or get rid of it. No reason even to maintain the person's name in your log or database. This group might

represent thirty to forty percent of all new contacts I make.

Priority 3: Save it in the database but give it low priority. Maybe in the future this will turn out to be a more valuable contact. But for now stick it away in your database and maybe include it when doing general-purpose updating e-marketing efforts. Maybe thirty-five percent of my new contacts fall in this category.

Priority 2: Potentially an important future contact. Put these in a group of people with whom you want to stay in touch on a fairly consistent basis, maybe once a quarter or once every six months. You definitely see longer-term value in this new relationship and want to nurture it over time. Possibly twenty percent of new contacts are a Priority 2.

Priority 1: A home run. These are the new contacts you absolutely want to develop a short-term, win-win relationship with and with anticipated long-term benefits. They have immediate potential ways that might benefit you and you have ways that you can contribute to their own personal and/or professional success. At most this is five percent of the new connections I make. This group probably won't have any more than fifty to a hundred names in it at any one time (out of the several thousand people you know), but they are your cream of the crop contacts. This is also a group that should be pruned and trimmed from time to time as circumstances change and newer contacts become more important, active, and relevant.

Make certain you practice networking every day, plus be well organized keeping track of your contacts with a database management system. A story illustrates the point.

Advising Mr. "W," a Captain of American Industry about His Private Investments

Back in the seventies, several years after I left McKinsey and struck out on my own, a recruiter contacted me (not sure why me) to see if I would be interested in meeting Mr. "W," one of the real captains in the history of American industry. He was certainly a titan at the time. He was one of the most impressive people I have ever met, and I respect his privacy and cannot reveal his name. Mr. "W" was looking for one person to work with him, as his partner, to manage his significant private investments in diverse companies. He had others managing other parts of his diversified portfolio in the stock market and real estate, for example.

To the person he eventually selected he was going to pay a handsome salary plus loan $2 million (a lot of money at the time) so the "partner" could co-invest with Mr. "W" on the same terms in the selected deals. When the partnership ended, for whatever reason, the person selected would be expected to repay the $2 million loan without interest. Any net gain from the partnership investments would be shared 90/10. Mr. "W" was going to put up a total of $20 million for this fund.

I jumped at the opportunity, recognizing I would be competing for the opportunity with some major league venture capital investment pros with backgrounds I could not hope to match.

My initial meeting with Mr."W" went well, I thought. He was one of the most impressive business leaders I have ever met. Note: My views on quality business leaders might be the subject of another book in the future.

To see how I would approach evaluating an investment opportunity, he asked me to do some research on a public tech company in which he had recently invested several million dollars. He had made the investment on the advice of his brother-in-law's investment advisor. The brother-in-law was also an earlier investor in the recommended company.

Back then, doing research of any kind was a real bear of a job

110

with about the only viable resources being the public libraries. This was before the Internet, search engines, phone apps, fax machines, cell phones, and cable TV. This was really back in the dark ages of communication. Going the route of trying to find relevant documents in the library would have taken weeks, if not months. I could not afford to spend most of my time on this nonpaying assignment while still trying to grow my own emerging venture, fundraising, and consulting company.

So, racking my brain, that same afternoon I decided to call Jim, head of a subsidiary of one of Mr. "W"'s companies and a previous McKinsey client of mine. Jim was in my networking database even though we had not communicated in years. Without telling him the reason for my call (I assumed Mr. "W" preferred to keep our discussions confidential), I wanted to see if Jim knew of the tech company in which Mr. "W" had invested and if he had an opinion and suggestion regarding how I could find out more about the company.

Jim reacted as if I'd hit him with an electric cattle prod. He immediately started ripping into the company: lousy products, poor customer service, way overpriced. You get the picture. The conversation took no more than five or ten minutes.

When I hung up, I realized I was onto how to do fast, reliable research on this investment. I started calling IT leaders in the other companies I had served while working with McKinsey, such as American Express, Burlington Great Northern Railway, Home Life Insurance, the Port of Philadelphia, and others. The feedback from all of these knowledgeable IT sources was equally negative. By the end of the same day as my initial meeting with Mr. "W," I knew what my conclusion and recommendation to him would be.

Note: Previously I mention how networking can actually be a time saver instead of a time drainer. Networking in one day among my IT contacts certainly saved me weeks of time I could have spent doing more traditional financial research and analysis.

First thing the next morning, I called Mr. "W" and arranged to meet him later that day. Our meeting lasted about twenty minutes. Without going into the details of how I got to my conclusion, I suggested he sell his invested position as quickly as possible despite the strong endorsement of this brother-in-law's financial advisor.

He asked me, "Are you sure?"

Absolutely, I said. "I don't think the company will do well. It may not survive." I could see that Mr. "W" was skeptical and thought I was shallow in doing important financial research and analysis. He was polite, but it was clear he was not impressed. I am sure I went to the end of the line among the people he was considering joining him in this important and fascinating new role.

A few months later, Mr. "W"'s secretary called and asked if I could come up for another lunch meeting. "Of course," I said. I already knew that the company's stock in which he had invested had cratered and was heading into Chapter 11. Now I had his attention.

Over lunch he asked me how I had managed to do such important analysis so quickly and so accurately. Without revealing names of the people I contacted, I basically told him I had reached out to key IT people in my network, ones likely to be current or potential customers of the tech company in which he had invested. He was intrigued with the fact that I had called the shot correctly and so quickly when the other candidates he was considering waffled on their conclusions. None of the other potential investing partners for Mr. "W" had said, "Cut your losses and get out."

From that point forward over the next few months, Mr. "W" asked me to evaluate other private investment opportunities he was considering. He didn't offer to pay me, and I didn't ask to be paid. We were both basically feeling each other out. We looked at a few other investment situations including an East Coast meat-packing company and a major retailer (you would recognize the name). In each case I managed to come back with unusual slants on how and why to make or not make an investment. Every time I reached out into my network to get relevant feedback on the opportunity.

I was willing to put in this time gratis because I viewed possibly working with Mr. "W" as a major potential opportunity in which it was worth investing some of my time. It was networking at the highest level.

After we looked at three or four possible deals together, Mr.

"W" finally offered me the opportunity to work with him as his partner making private investments in companies he or we turned up and found interesting and viable. His offer was mind-boggling, fair, and generous. If we had succeeded together, I would have been set for life.

Unfortunately there was one stumbling block that I felt strongly about and he did as well. We couldn't reach agreement on this issue, so I reluctantly turned down the offer and walked away from the relationship. It was one of the toughest career-altering business decisions I ever made, but it was the right one from my perspective. Mr. "W" was obviously equally upset that we had come so far and yet reached an impasse. We never talked again. Maybe the reason will be in my next book but it basically revolved around my wanting to bring my two partners with me into this new opportunity, and Mr. "W" feeling strongly that he only wanted to work with one person in this new role.

Ask for the Connections You Need

Sometimes you must simply just ask for the kind of connections you need. Even though you want to position yourself as a giver, sometimes it just pays to ask others you know to introduce you to their resources that you would appreciate and value. A word of advice: only ask for referrals from people who know you well and respect you and your abilities.

Recently I was giving a networking coaching workshop to twenty women CPAs who are members of their national firm's women's initiative. To emphasize that every group situation is in essence a "network" and to demonstrate the power of being involved in a networking group, we asked everyone to stand and ask for one specific type of connection that would benefit them, personally.

It was amazing the range of resources members of the group were asking for and it was even more amazing how others in the group immediately started offering relevant connections. Some were looking for help losing weight. Another wanted to find a good dentist near where she lived. One wanted someone who could help her boyfriend, now two years out of college and still unable to land a job. Another wanted a piano instructor for her daughter. Still another wanted to find a nonprofit board on which she could serve.

The electricity in the group was amazing. I am sure all the participants immediately saw the power of networking in asking for help and sharing resources.

Network Your Way, at Your Pace

There is no right or wrong way to be effective at networking and developing relationships. You are totally in control of the process that works for you. These efforts need not and should not seriously interfere with your normal lifestyle. You can constantly modify your networking efforts based on the other things going on in your life. You decide how much time per week you want to devote to these activities. You decide when (mornings, lunch, evenings, weekday, or weekend) you will invest time and other resources in talking and meeting people.

You decide if you want to concentrate your networking efforts in one-on-one meetings or at events, in groups, or even online. You decide which of your clusters of connections you want to zoom in on with your networking efforts.

My basic approach is to meet people for breakfast five times a week (maybe six or seven times in some weeks) and spend an average of an hour at each meeting starting and developing relationships. You can do more or less. But at a minimum, I think most people with serious career ambitions should be spending five hours a week or more networking. For others with a pressing need such as trying to find a job or raise money for a new venture, networking forty to fifty hours a week, or more, may be needed. You control how you go about it.

At lunchtime, take a break, just get up out of your chair and get out of your office. Go meet someone for lunch or for a quick coffee break. Or go walk in the park and start talking to people you meet along the way.

I recently headed a three-hour networking workshop for New Jersey members of WAVE, Verizon's employee organization, with the majority of the members being primarily female engineering and management professionals. The question came up about how I spent my networking time. I sketched out on a whiteboard the following time-and-money analysis of my estimated annual networking efforts.

Jack's Estimated Annual Time and Money Invested in Networking

Networking Activities	Times/Year	Hours/Year	$$ Spent/Year
Breakfast Meetings	250	300	$5,000
Lunch Meetings	10	20	$450
Afternoon Coffee	6	12	$120
Dinner Meetings	4	10	$400
Attending Events	3	10	$225
In Group Meetings	5	15	$250
Driving for Meetings	To All Meetings	220	$3,500
Total	278	587	$9,945

Notes:

• Some 87% of my networking meetings a year are breakfast meetings that account for 51% of total time I spend networking annually.

• Another 37% of my networking-related time is spent driving to and from various meetings with most of the driving spent on breakfast meetings.

• I estimate 70 to 75% of the total time I spend networking per year, including driving time, happens before 9:00 or 9:30 a.m., leaving the rest of my day open.

• Assume the dollars spent annually on my networking efforts include my picking up every tab. That happens most of the time but not all of the time.

• In total, I invest less than $10,000/year developing and harvesting my substantial network. Part of the money is spent feeding me, which I would spend anyway even if not networking.

When appropriate, it is okay to involve your family members in your networking efforts. In an earlier chapter, when I was listing challenges people have relative to networking, I listed lack of time.

Undoubtedly that's an issue for all of us. One way I found that works is to involve my wife and our son in some of my networking efforts. Almost from the time Jonathan was born, I have taken him to my work activities. I brought him to my office first in a basket that I sat on top of my desk and then set up a crib and then a playpen in my office. I could do this obviously because I owned and headed the companies at the time. But I would have permitted others to do the same thing as long as it was not a big distraction. Some employees did, in fact, occasionally bring their kids to work with them. Having kids around always gave the mood in the company a boost.

I also took Jonathan to many business meetings I attended. I have positive experiences many times both in the United States and internationally when Jonathan tagged along to a meeting. In fact, I have never had a bad reaction to the two of us showing up.

It's even easier for me to involve Judy in most meetings. Since I do much of my networking over eggs in the morning, I often ask Judy if she wants to come along. In most cases, the people I am meeting enjoy also meeting Judy and learning a bit about her work empowering women through her Garden State Woman Education Foundation.

If I know we are going to be discussing something sensitive to the person I am meeting, I still might bring Judy along with the understanding that after the introduction, she will need to park herself at another table or booth and read the papers or a book or do some of her own work while I have my meeting.

At least she is getting treated to eggs and is getting to know the people with whom I am networking, and they are getting to see a personal side of me, which often can be a good thing in developing relationships. More couples should think about involving each other in their networking efforts although care needs to be taken that it is done appropriately and under the right circumstances.

Finally, practice, practice, practice and learn, learn, learn. We can all improve our networking skills and improve our ability to develop strong relationships and accelerate our careers and the profitable growth of the businesses for which we work.

So every day, practice. Talk with everyone you meet, anywhere, anytime.

Exceptional networkers do not live in their own little cocoons. Make talking with people another part of your lifestyle. It need not disrupt anything else you are doing.

And keep learning. There are excellent books on all aspects of networking and developing successful relationships and converting those relationships into new, profitable business and career opportunities. Besides this book, my favorite networking book is Never Eat Alone by Keith Ferrazzi and Tahl Raz.

YouTube and TED Talks have plenty of excellent videos on relevant aspects of what I am talking about in this book. Networking is a hot topic in our business society. There are plenty of networking events for you to attend and networking groups for you to join. Later on I deal specifically with networking at events and in groups.

Chapter Five

The Art of the Cold Call. Don't Be a Wimp. Get Over Your Fears. Suck it Up

I don't know anyone who likes to cold call. Do you? I certainly don't. Even most pros at it, people who earn their living cold calling, would prefer spending their time other ways. Sometimes, though, you just have to suck it up and reach out cold if you want or need to get to somebody potentially important to you personally or professionally.

Often, when you are under the gun time-wise and have to go after your goal quickly and decisively, cold calling is the fastest, most direct and only route to a connection you need.

What exactly is cold calling? Cold calling to me means having the need to reach someone important to you at the time and not having any clear, simple way to get to the targeted new connection in a stress-free way. A few personal examples follow.

My early cold calling days go back to when I quit my consulting job with McKinsey & Company to strike out on my own. That really was stepping off the ledge. I was so committed to seeing if I could survive and thrive entrepreneurially that I left McKinsey with only a vague idea of what I would pursue as a new career. Please don't do this. In retrospect I should have thought through things a bit more, although I probably would have made the same decision. But back then, I was young and semi confident that I could make it (whatever "it" would turn out to be).

When I resigned from McKinsey, I lacked any relevant, important contacts. I didn't have any employees or partners teaming up with me. I didn't have any clients or potential clients. I didn't have an office (other than the kitchen table) or even business cards! And I certainly didn't have a nest egg, wealthy parents, or investors to fall back on. It was sink-or-swim time.

I basically just decided that I would pursue my passion for working with small companies helping them grow and develop. I grew up in a tiny family-owned tool and die business, Killion Tool & Die Manufacturing Company. I watched my dad with his lack of funding and only an eighth-grade education bootstrap his way to a modestly successful career until a year or two before he passed. In my early years he was my hero and role model. For my master's thesis at MIT, I wrote on the challenges of owning and developing small businesses. Being an entrepreneur has been in my blood. It's a part of my DNA.

The informal business model I decided to follow was twofold. I would help owners of high-potential small businesses raise needed funding for growth while providing them management guidance and direction. I would also help investors in high-potential emerging and/ or troubled companies develop and implement strategies for profitably growing or turning them around. I was sure there were plenty of potential clients in both categories. Unfortunately, on day one I didn't have any of either type of client, and I wasn't sure where I was going to get either.

Compounding the challenges of finding and landing paying clients was the absence, at the time, of easy ways to reach people. As I said earlier, back then there was the phone and US mail system. That was basically it. There were no fax machines, cell phones, laptops, e-mail, Google, LinkedIn, Facebook, or networking events and groups.

The Art of the Cold Call.
Don't Be a Wimp. Get Over Your Fears. Suck it Up

I knew that I was going to have to cold call my way to people as the process for developing a base of revenue-producing clients. I hated—and I mean hated—cold calling people, but that was what I had to do. I had no choice.

So every day I would leave home with pounds of change, mostly quarters, bulging my pockets. I knew I would be spending a good part of the day trying to get through to people on pay phones in New York's Grand Central Station or in hotel lobbies. I absolutely hated it. I was deathly afraid to pick up the phone to make the call. I usually would let the phone ring two or three times and, if no answer, hang up with my sweaty palm, almost thankful that I had not been connected.

Since I had little choice, I kept cold calling starting primarily with institutional investors I could identify who might be interested in learning about a deal if I ever landed a client company looking for fresh capital. I called banks, insurance companies, pension funds, Wall Street leaders, and wealthy families and their foundations such as the Rockefellers, Phipps, Fords, and the Rothschilds. My objective was always to arrange a meeting so I could learn exactly the type of investments they would consider. Back then I was much better dealing in person than by phone. I am still very much that way today.

I learned that every sophisticated, successful investor has their own specific investment objectives. Some like start-ups. Some like technology deals. Others like real estate opportunities. Others will look at turnarounds. Some will look at smaller companies. Some will not. Some will want to make equity investments. Others will want to only lend their funds. Some want only US-based opportunities. Others will take on international projects.

Eventually I got through to people and had my meetings. I learned a couple of important lessons. Generally the easier it was to get through, the higher the quality of the person. It was the middle-of-the-road person who felt he or she was a big shot with a lot of power who tended to give me a tough time or totally ignore my calls.

To this day I am totally indebted to the then managing director of New Court Securities, the US venture capital investing arm of the Rothschild family. He was totally receptive to meeting and generous with his time and his guidance. There were others willing to help me, an emerging entrepreneur, by outlining their investing objectives and processes. Jack Dreyfus, founder of the Dreyfus Funds, was another who quickly agreed to meet and share his investment objectives and requirements.

I eventually started building a fairly robust network among heavy-hitting investment professionals and developing an understanding of exactly the types of potential investments they would consider. The range of their investment interests was amazing.

Then an unexpected benefit started to develop. I started getting calls from emerging company business owners looking to raise capital. Most were being referred to me by my new institutional and high-net-worth individual investor contacts. Rather than simply rejecting an opportunity because it didn't fit their criteria, they started saying, "Why don't you call Jack. Maybe he can help." The pool of my potential investors started becoming sources of potential deals I could look at and possibly help. My early connections started sharing their contacts with me.

As we started to get to know each other better, some of the investors groups started asking me if my firm could help them think through how to turn around troubled companies in which they had invested earlier.

Within a few months of going off on my own, I had two partners join me. Both had been clients of mine with McKinsey. Both had strong educational backgrounds. Russ Barnard also went to Yale, and Spencer Oettinger graduated from Brown University. Both had substantial successful work experience in diverse industries. The three of us were a formidable team, feeling quite capable of tackling major investing and turnaround projects.

We worked together in this role for five years before moving on to raise capital and start our own venture, publishing Country Music magazine.

It was during this initial five-year period of being on my own that I cut my teeth learning to successfully cold call. I never learned to love doing it, but, when push comes to shove, I am capable of making important cold calls. The learning curve has also taught me to respect and be more patient with people trying to cold call me. I can always afford a minute or two to listen to someone's reason for calling before deciding go or no-go regarding continuing the conversation and maybe agreeing to meet.

Some Personal Cold Calling Examples to Start a Magazine, Buy a Farm. Meet the Yankee's Pitching Coach, and Initiate a Connection to the White House

Five years after starting my initial company, Killion Barnard & Oettinger (KBO), to raise funding for client businesses, the three of us decided our business model, while certainly an exciting way to learn about hundreds of diverse businesses and sharpen our analytical and entrepreneurial skills, was a tough way to earn a living. We decided, if we were so smart and capable, why not raise capital to start and grow our own business?

Because Texas-born and -raised Russ Barnard, one of my KBO partners, had previously held a key marketing role at Columbia Records, and we had looked at many publishing deals and had a small hand in the early stage development of Rolling Stone magazine, we decided to start America's first national country music magazine.

One day, while still thinking through how to raise $500,000 to start Country Music magazine (that was its name), we saw an article in the New York Times talking about Harper's magazine having some difficulties. That triggered us to cold call the chairman of the Minneapolis Star & Tribune Company, owners of Harper's, and eventually propose a two-part working relationship. Just out of the blue, we called him. And look where it got us.

We would be retained to manage Harper's and hopefully get it through the difficult days and positioned to be sold. The Minneapolis Star & Tribune would also put up the $500,000 and own half the equity in the new Country Music magazine we wanted to start. After several meetings over just a few weeks in New York and at their Midwest headquarters, we got that two-part deal done.

In its second year, Country Music was the second-fastest-growing consumer magazine in the country. Only People Magazine grew faster. Country Music was published for well over twenty-five years, long past our exit point.

Harper's was eventually sold and the Minneapolis Star & Tribune Company profitably sold their stake in Country Music back to the three of us.

Here's another example of how I raised the money to buy our fifty-acre farm to breed and raise race horses

When my dad passed, he owned a fifty-acre farm in New Jersey, which he used unsuccessfully to breed and race thoroughbred race horses. In his will, his executors were instructed to sell the farm and use the proceeds to create a trust for my mom, my dad's other kids, and his grandchildren. The executors quickly lined up several possible buyers and had a firm letter of intent.

Judy and I had thirty days to match the highest offer. We wanted to buy the farm but had almost no money, certainly not nearly enough to buy a prime property in northern New Jersey. Days went by as we racked our brains for a solution.

Then one day I was in Kentucky on a trip to sell advertising in Country Music to the cigarette companies. The receptionist at one of the companies kept me waiting and stewing. Then an idea struck me. Why not cold call the US Secretary of Agriculture and ask him how someone could raise money quickly to buy a farm versus letting it go into development. I assumed the Department of Agriculture would prefer maintaining a farm as a farm instead of letting it go into another housing development. The Liggett & Myers receptionist let me use the phone in their waiting area. She was probably feeling sorry about how long I had been sitting there.

I made the cold call. I never got through to the Secretary of Agriculture, but I did get passed onto one of his key assistants who, in fact, confirmed that the Department of Agriculture did have programs to help fund the acquisition of farms. Given my description of our finances, the size of the deal, and our plans for using the farm, he told me about how much I could expect to raise quickly through government programs. He outlined the process we needed to follow and connected me with the right person in New Jersey who could guide us through the government maze.

That still left us with a significant gap in the funding we needed to complete the purchase within the thirty-day deadline.

The next day, when I got home, I called our partner investor in Country Music, the Minneapolis Star & Tribune Company. I outlined the funding problem and farm purchase goal that we had. I asked if their company would buy out my equity in Country Music for the amount of the gap in funding we faced. We both knew the value of my equity in the magazine was worth significantly more than I was asking for in the sale of my stake in the company.

The chairman called me the following day to tell me a check for the amount we needed was in the overnight mail but that they wanted to structure it as a loan and not as an equity buyout. They were happy with my performance running both magazines and concerned that if I didn't have a piece of the equity in Country Music, that I might lose my enthusiasm and commitment. That would not have happened. I loved the projects and the industry. But we did the transaction as a loan the way they preferred. Judy and I worked as quickly as possible to repay it, which we did. We still live on Walnut Farm. I am writing this book sitting in my barn office!

Here is yet another story of how I networked our son through a cold contact to the pitching coach of the Yankees.

When Jonathan was younger, he was an excellent Little League baseball player. He pitched, played shortstop, and switch hit. He was way above average as a ball player.

One summer Judy took him on one of their summer trips in our Ford pickup truck to Alaska. Judy was committed to getting Jonathan to visit all forty-nine states in our Ford pickup. This took them four summers to accomplish. They closed out seeing America by flying and spending four weeks in Hawaii. The Alaskan trip in our pickup was the longest. I missed them a great deal.

I wanted to do something special for Jonathan when they got home. So I got the crazy idea of trying to get Jonathan to meet and talk pitching with Russ Meyers, at the time, the pitching coach of the New York Yankees. I am a lifelong Yankee fan.

I didn't have anybody who could connect me with Mr. Meyers, so I sent him a cold call type letter well in advance of Judy and Jonathan getting home. I simply asked if he would be willing to meet and talk conditioning and pitching with Jonathan. He called the same day he got the letter and said he would be more than happy to meet Jonathan when he came back from his Alaskan trip.

Spending the better part of a day having Mr. Myers and Jonathan talk pitching and having Jonathan meet some of the Yankee ball players is certainly among the top few things I have ever accomplished. Russ Meyers turned out to be just an awesome human being. He stayed in touch with Jonathan by phone and mail for several years before he passed.

Here's how I got on the White House radar screen by getting a state senator to pass a copy of Country Music magazine to President Richard Nixon.

The day we published the first issue of Country Music magazine with Johnny Cash on the cover, we were so excited and pumped to share our "success."

The next day, after an evening of celebrating with too much sangria, we sent by registered mail a copy of Country Music to Senator Bill Brock of Tennessee, whom we had never met, asking him to forward it to President Nixon, whom we learned was a country music fan. Shortly after sending the copy, I received a hand-delivered, personalized letter dated September 25, 1972, from President Nixon thanking me for the copy and saying how much he enjoyed the Johnny Cash story. The letter is framed along with the cover of the first issue of the magazine issue and is hanging on my Walnut Farm barn office wall.

When President Nixon was invited to open the new Grand Old Opry at Opryland after it moved from the old Ryman auditorium in downtown Nashville, I was invited to be part of the press party covering the event and having access to the president.

Years later, when Jimmy Carter was elected president, his campaign benefited significantly from the money-raising efforts of the country music industry that supported his run for president. He had a special thank-you dinner at the White House for the leading performers and executives in the industry.

As the publisher of the country music industry's leading consumer publication, I was included on the guest list. One of my more memorable experiences was spending quality one-on-one time talking with President Carter at the White House. One of my questions that really struck a chord with him was when I asked him, "How many exceptional, difference-making people do you have helping you run the government?"

Before answering, he asked me for my guess. One day hopefully I will have a chance to share both answers with you! My guess was twice as many as President Carter's answer.

The day after visiting the White House for President Carter's event, I sent him a thank-you note along with separate gifts for him, his wife, and his daughter. A few days later a hand-delivered letter from President Carter showed up thanking me for the gifts.

This trail to two US presidents was triggered by my reaching out cold to President Nixon via a letter to the Tennessee state senator with a copy of the first issue of Country Music.

THE WHITE HOUSE

WASHINGTON

September 25, 1972

Dear Mr. Killion:

Bill Brock passed along to me a copy of
COUNTRY MUSIC. Needless to say, I
enjoyed the opportunity of reading your
magazine, especially the account of
Johnny Cash's performance here, and I
join with your readers in congratulating
you and all the staff of COUNTRY MUSIC
on this first issue.

With my best wishes for continued success,

Sincerely,

Richard Nixon

Mr. Jack Killion
Publisher
COUNTRY MUSIC
Suite 1102
500 Fifth Avenue
New York, New York 10036

THE WHITE HOUSE

WASHINGTON

May 9, 1978

To Jack Killion

Thank you for your warm message.

Rosalynn and I were pleased that you could attend
our Country Music Reception last month, and we
appreciate your thoughtfulness in sending us and
Amy the specially designed "Country Music"
mementos.

You were also kind to arrange for us to receive
your magazine. I know we will enjoy reading it.

With best wishes,

Sincerely,

Jimmy

Mr. Jack Killion
President and Publisher
Country Music Magazine
475 Park Avenue South
New York, New York 10016

In 2001 I teamed up with a since-long-gone partner to launch Eagle Rock Diversified Fund. It was developed primarily to invest capital from family and friends into a diversified portfolio of hedge funds.

Investing in hedge funds is not for all investors. There are over twelve thousand hedge funds globally to choose from. Most investors know little about this alternative asset form of investing. It took the two of us nearly a year to get comfortable with the concept of starting our own fund-of-funds and raising capital from other investors to be invested in a collection of hedge funds that we selected and monitored.

As with any start-up fund-of-funds, we knew that credibility was critical for both raising capital and for gaining access into world-class hedge funds.

One way for two newcomers to the industry like us to create some credibility was to surround ourselves with the best professional advisors we could find. We knew picking the right accountant and right accounting firm to work with us to prepare our annual audits and tax returns would be critical.

After some due diligence, we identified Peter Testaverde, a partner heading the hedge fund practice with GGK. At the time, Peter was one of the most respected accountants in the US hedge fund industry and still enjoys that same exceptional reputation fifteen years later.

We reached out cold to Peter who, given he was living in New Jersey, agreed to meet us at Harold's Diner in Parsippany one morning for eggs and a discussion.

To make a long story short, Peter not only agreed his firm would be our audit and tax accountants, he also agreed to start out giving us a break on fees while we gained traction. He also referred us to Jeff Cobb, the Connecticut lawyer that Peter recommended we use for the fund's legal work. We benefited enormously from the credibility that Peter and Jeff helped create for us in the early years. I am sure those relationships helped us both raise capital and gain access into some of the world's best hedge funds.

Without Peter and Jeff as our early professional advisors, I doubt our fund-of-funds would have ever gotten off the ground.

My partner, when we launched the fund, resigned after a few years for health reasons. With my son, Jonathan, as another general partner for the past few years, I continue managing the Eagle Rock Diversified Fund, which is still invested in two of the first three hedge funds we went into back in 2001. Two of our first three investors remain in the fund fourteen years later.

Bottom line about cold calling: I could go on and give more examples about my personal successful cold calling experiences as well as those of others, but I am sure you get the picture.

Today, totally cold calling is seldom necessary. Modern communication makes it easy to connect with people globally. LinkedIn and Facebook are two tools that facilitate the process of being connected with others we don't know personally.

But at some points throughout your personal and business life, you are going to have to suck it up and make a cold call or two. E-mail certainly makes this process much less stressful. I found it works. People often will respond to cold e-mails. If that fails, pick up the phone!

If it is important enough, you will do whatever is required to connect with the person you need to reach.

My Bulldog George Is a Proven Icebreaker

I recently took a quick trip to Maine for a family celebration and brought George, our bulldog, along. We have always owned dogs like Shepherds, Scotties, English Setters and others but never a bulldog.

I was amazed at how many people approached me just to ask about and pet George. People with kids or their own dogs were particularly attracted to George and wanted to talk. I could have met as many new and interesting people as I wanted simply sitting on a bench in the harbor town of Camden, Maine, or staying at the dog-friendly B&B we found.

I could go on with a long list of the people we met for the first time, many of whom are turning out to be potentially important personal or business connections.

For example, we met:

• *A senior VP with UnitedHealthcare who has a possible interest in her company using our networking training firm*

• *A performing pianist who invited us to a concert that Saturday night in Rockport*

• *A woodworker and competitive paddle boarder who invited us to watch a race he was in the next day—an entirely new world for me*

• *A bookstore owner who saw me walking George out front and came out to welcome us into his store. He invited me to come back that evening for a book signing by a local author. By time we got done starting to build our new relationship, he was suggesting I come back up to Maine for a book signing for this book!*

George also caught the attention of a former US Senator now living in Maine who turned out to have a strong interest in the work being done by the Garden State Woman Education Foundation to empower high school girls and disadvantaged inner-city women. We are scheduling a follow-up meeting to discuss possible synergies with his own foundation.

The point is, if you have a people-friendly dog, recognize that they can be really good at helping you initiate new, potentially important and exciting relationships.

The final piece of cold calling advice: When you really have to make a key connection, and there are no other options, just plow ahead. Practice what you are going to say to get through the gatekeeper and then get on it. Nobody bites, not even the mean, miserable people. If you are persistent (you may have to call a few times), have a legitimate reason for calling, can get your legitimate request out in twenty to thirty seconds, then you are going to get through and hopefully get to where you want to go. You will be amazed at how many gatekeepers, when asked nicely for their help, will help.

Sometimes you get the best results by just showing up at the person's location and, using all of your charm, simply asking if your target contact can spare a few minutes since you are in the area.

Chapter Six

Get Belly-to-Belly

Originally this chapter was called Networking One-on-One, but then in various ways the most effective networking comes down to one-on-one, belly-to-belly communication. That's how the most important long-term relationships are developed. The benefits of networking this way will never be replaced by text messaging and social media.

The three basic types of networking are

- Serendipitous

- In clusters

- Targeted

Serendipitous Networking

I want you to realize that chance meetings, the serendipitous kind, can lead to new important connections and relationships in your network and new joint opportunities. This goes back to talking everywhere, all the time, with everyone. It is spontaneous and interferes little time-wise with your other activities.

Serendipitous networking:

• Is not planned. It just happens as you go through each day.

• Is a series of random chance meetings, lacking any preconceived goals.

• Usually happens quickly, often lasting only a minute or a few minutes. These are "glancing" meetings.

• Can lead to mutually good things and a more extended relationship if you do ask probing questions and quickly find out about the other person—that is, finding the common touch points between you.

• Leads to a more substantial relationship generating mutual benefits only a small portion of the time (maybe five or ten percent at most).

• Is a low-risk, low-cost, low-return way to meet new people and possibly to begin building new relationships. It is also a strong way to get more comfortable talking with people.

The payback from excelling at casually meeting new people, striking up impromptu conversations, and learning to do a better job of quickly finding out about the other person is that the technique is a training ground for doing the planned and targeted networking that you need to focus on to generate most of your most important personal and professional results.

Here are a few quick examples of fortuitous, serendipitous networking experiences I have had that yielded important outcomes.

Starting a Hedge Fund

One evening I stopped at a local pub on the way home for a beer and sandwich at the bar. Already sitting there when I arrived was a woman waiting for her physician husband to show up for dinner. We started talking. Turns out she was a senior VP/investment advisor at one of America's top Wall Street firms.

As we talked and started to learn more about our backgrounds, she mentioned that she was thinking of starting a hedge fund and asked if I might have an interest in joining her in the project. At the time I was publisher and editor of Wireless for the Corporate User magazine and deeply involved in all the new mobile and wireless communications technologies coming on stream. That was probably the first time I had ever heard the words hedge fund. We agreed to meet again in a week at her office in New York.

Cutting right to the bottom line, within a year I had learned a lot about the hedge fund industry and believed that my new "friend" had the skill set to manage a hedge fund portfolio. We agreed to team up to launch a new hedge fund focusing on the emerging information and communications tech sector—the dot.com era.

My new partner was to focus on investing the assets. My main role was to attract investors to the fund. We did well for a couple of years until the tech bubble burst. Needing to change our business model, we agreed to close the fund and offer the investors either to withdraw their investment that remained or to roll their capital over into a more general-purpose hedge fund that my "partner" was developing without my ongoing involvement. I wanted to go in a different direction. And so we parted.

That chance meeting at a local pub over a beer and sandwich was a major shaper of my life for fifteen years.

Framing Pictures

I was in a local shop one evening framing some horse-racing prints and winning photos. This was back when Judy and I were heavily involved in the thoroughbred racing industry and had our own Walnut Farm breeding and racing stable.

Shortly after I started framing that night, Steve and David, two brothers, came over and started talking with me about the prints and photos I was framing. Our conversation quickly turned to their interest as fans and my involvement as a breeder, owner, and trainer in the racing industry.

We had a great couple of hours framing and talking. It was obvious that the brothers had a deep interest in racing as devoted fans. They were aware of my racing involvement from seeing my name as trainer in the programs whenever we ran a horse at a New Jersey, Pennsylvania, or New York track. They were enthusiastic meeting someone like me (even though in the overall scheme of things in the racing industry, I was just a bit player!) with as much experience as I had in an area of their strong interest. We hit it off immediately.

A couple of weeks later, David and Steve called to say they were considering buying a race horse that was recuperating at a farm after being injured (not badly) at the track. They asked if I would be willing to look at the horse for them. They offered to pay for my time. Having found two such quality guys so interested in a sport I loved dearly at the time, I told them no need to pay me. I would be happy to take a look at the horse and tell them what I thought.

We went together to check out the horse. My conclusion was, "It is just another horse." There was no real way to tell whether or not it would ever turn out to be okay at the track. The breeding was nothing special. I think David and Steve were disappointed that I was not encouraging them to go ahead and make the purchase. Instead I told them racing is a tough, complex, and always expensive sport.

For newcomers, without any real firsthand experience, I told them it would be a huge risk for them to get involved. I suggested a better next step would be for me to get them licensed to work with me at the tracks and to have them come mornings on the weekends and on their days off to watch and get involved in what goes on in the racing world. This would be their interning opportunity to build up their knowledge in the industry.

We spent time together on this basis for a few years with their getting involved in our racing stable. They learned to walk, feed, and generally care for horses. They learned how to deal with other trainers, jockeys, jockey agents, vets, blacksmiths, feed and hay suppliers, and racing officials. They learned the business. Finally, when I thought they were ready, I suggested they buy a small percentage of a horse owned and trained by Jeff, a good friend of the three of us, so they could participate as owners.

I had them keep the percentage low in case the horse didn't work out. I wanted to minimize their potential losses while at the same time giving them a real opportunity to share in the ups and downs of racing as owners. Fortunately, the horse Slanky turned out to be decent and the partnership worked. Their modest infusion of cash into Jeff's small racing stable also helped him cover the costs of getting the horse ready to start his racing career.

It is now at least twenty-five years later, and we are all still best of friends. We have seen each other's kids grow up, go to college, and get into the workforce. We have spent time with our wives sharing another common passion, finding exceptional out-of-the-way restaurants.

Steve's son David was hooked with thoroughbred racing at a very early age when he started coming to our farm to see our horses. Today, young David is a couple of years out of NYU, has a nice job in marketing with a major New York performing arts center, and has his own highly regarded racing blog at thatsahorsetowatch.com.

Earlier this year I suggested David Sr. get involved in an advisory role in PeopleProductive, another emerging company in which I am active. This company I believe will emerge as a global leader in boosting productivity of the workforce by assessing, monitoring, and improving organizational cultures.

The benefits of a chance meeting twenty-five years ago are still compounding.

Riding the Train

Riding the crowded train into Manhattan one morning I was sitting next to a young woman who worked on her laptop the entire trip while wearing ear buds listening to young people's music. We never said a word the entire trip until just before we pulled into Penn Station when she closed down the Apple computer and took the things out of her ears.

I asked, "What have you been working so hard on this whole trip?"

She explained she was finishing up an unpaid internship at a New York marketing agency as a graphic designer. I asked if she could quickly reboot her computer and show me examples of her work. What I saw was enough to convince me that she had real talent, so I asked for her business card so I could follow up. I am always involved with projects that can benefit from having some excellent graphic design. She didn't have a business card, violating one of the key factors for success when networking. I gave her one of mine and told her of some of the things in which I am involved. I suggested she reach out if she was interested in meeting.

Jessica e-mailed me later that week, and we agreed to meet for coffee one morning. In that hour I got to see more of her design work. She learned more about what I do. We broke up the meeting with Jessica agreeing to do some design work for me and my projects and for my wife's Garden State Woman Education Foundation. Jessica needed real-life examples for her portfolio that was required to land the type of job she wanted. We obviously agreed to let her use the work she did for us as part of her portfolio, and we also offered to connect her with people in our networks who might be looking for a part-time or full-time graphic designer.

Within a week we had plugged her into five possible viable job possibilities. I also learned that her parents have their own family law practice in Florida. Jessica has been helping them with their website and other graphic needs.

As this book is going to the publisher, Jessica is sorting through the various opportunities we introduced her to, and we are using some of her initial designs in our own projects and have her working on other more robust projects. We have also suggested various resources to Jessica that her parents might use to drive their own law practice. Our networking coaching firm works with professionals in many law firms, so we have developed a quiver of ideas and resources that these firms use to grow their practices. I am sure this relationship will go on for a long time. Jessica is the quality of person we identify with easily.

The point is this: start talking with everyone. Serendipitously, important things will often happen.

Cluster Networking

Besides networking serendipitously, most of us who work hard to develop our careers and empower our families tend to do quality networking within our clusters of connections.

Depending on our lifestyles and career paths, we all have our own unique clusters of people with whom we generally spend time—our network. A typical cluster of relationships might include family, friends, neighbors, college alumni, high school friends, fellow club members, colleagues within the organization, professional external contacts including clients, suppliers, and advisors.

It is within these clusters that we all spend most of our time. They provide much of the richness we enjoy in our careers and in our

141

personal lives.

Our clusters of connections can vary at different points in our lives, and we can elect at any point to put more or less emphasis on any one or more of the clusters. For example, twenty years ago two of my heavily accessed clusters would have been in the thoroughbred racing and country music industries, both of which were important to my career and lifestyle at the time.

Today, I spend almost no time with people in either of these groups but have replaced these clusters with people I have met and developed relationships with within the hedge fund, professional coaching industries, universities, and entrepreneurs.

We often ask our networking coaching clients how many contacts they have in their network. The answers we generally get are almost always fewer than five hundred.

If people stopped and thought a minute about the various clusters of people with whom they come into contact, they would realize their in-person connections number in the thousands, not in the hundreds.

The key take-away point here is that, within your individual and unique clusters of contacts, you have people likely positioned to help you achieve whatever professional and personal goal you pursue at the time.

Networking in clusters is much more productive than networking serendipitously. If you cobble together and focus on the "right" people in your clusters, then you will have enormous untapped potential to draw on when you are going after a specific personal or business goal.

The more robust your clusters of connections, the greater your chances of developing and enjoying an exceptional professional career and personal and family life.

Targeted Networking

Targeted networking is geared to achieving specific objectives.

It is by far the most productive way to spend networking efforts if you have specific, clear, well-defined professional and personal goals.

Targeted networking involves:

• Having a goal, an objective. What is the purpose of making the connection? The goal can be personal, such as meeting a future spouse or getting to play an exclusive golf course or finding the right resource for adopting a child, or it can be career or business related, such as finding a new job, finding an investor for a new venture, recruiting a new leader for the company, or finding a new strategic alliance in another country.

• Listing, under the goal, specific people/organizations or specific type of people/organizations you need to connect with in order to accomplish your goal.

• Learning as much as you can in advance about the person and about their organization. Besides arming yourself with information that can be critically important during your conversation or meeting, it is disrespectful not to do your homework in advance when meeting someone for the first time.

• Having a strategy and plan for making a connection with the specific people or organizations you need to reach to achieve your objective. You can get to your target connections either by cold calling or, more likely, by going through your clusters of contacts to find one or more to link you to the connection you need to make.

A CEO Did Not Do Her Homework

A few years ago Judy asked me to do a phone interview for

a cover story for her Garden State Woman magazine, the leading magazine in New Jersey at the time for professional and corporate women. Because of my business and real estate development background, I was interviewing a woman who owned and headed one of the largest real estate development firms in the country. She was heading a major development along the Hudson River in New Jersey. Her PR firm had been after Judy for months to do a cover story on their client.

The first few minutes of my phone interview was not going well. I thought the real estate developer was not clear on what we were doing. So I asked, "Why do you want to be interviewed by Garden State Woman magazine?"

Her answer stunned me: "I don't know anything about the magazine. My PR firm just asked me to be available for an interview this afternoon."

Needless to say, I cut off the conversation and suggested she do some homework on Judy's company and magazine. We never heard from her or the PR firm again, although I did threaten our contact at the agency with telling his boss what a poor job he had done preparing their client for an important cover story interview. I am a softie and never followed through on my threat. I think he got the message.

Helping a Struggling College Graduate Find Her First Job

I recently was asked to help a friend's college graduate daughter find her first job out of college. She had graduated over a year ago, leaving college without a job—a real indictment against the university, I think!

Before we met, I asked to see her resume, which showed her objective as this: "To become a part of a company that values professionalism and integrity, while challenging and motivating me every day."

I thought that was a noble kind of objective, but, from a potential employer's point of view, I wasn't certain what that meant. When we met,

I told Rachel that, in her objective statement, she needed to be much more specific about what type of job she was looking for. She had difficulty defining what she would write instead.

We talked through a multistep process I like to use in these situations. I asked her to do the following:

- *Define her skills and experiences she would bring to a new job. She listed some college-based marketing experience, extensive international travel and studying abroad, strong writing skills, and strong social media skills. These were key attributes she could bring to a new situation. Knowing your skill set and aptitudes can sharpen your job search.*

- *List her passions and areas of interest. After much hemming and hawing, she finally listed five areas of strong personal interest she cared about: music, animals, ice cream, international hospitality, and fashion. It seemed to me Rachel should focus on finding a job with leading organizations in these sectors that reflected her core passions and interests. Why ever work in an industry or an organization that just does not excite you?*

- *Identify organizations in each area of interest and passion that she would like to research and potentially put on her hit list of potential employers to target.*

Within days she had developed a grid of possible organizations she felt she would feel proud to join and enjoy working with in sectors she found particularly interesting.

- *Develop a series of resumes with each matching the potential needs of the preselected targeted companies.*

- *Flush out her LinkedIn profile, the first place probably that any potential new employer is going to go to check her out. It needed to be top notch.*

• *Identify all the various clusters of connections that she has and can tap into for referrals to key people in her target companies. She listed her extended family, neighbors, and others in her community, high school, and college connections (other students, their parents, faculty, guest lecturers), previous employer connections, study abroad connections, sorority connections, and LinkedIn connections. She started reaching out.*

• *Before resorting to cold calling, she would start networking among current cluster connections looking for referrals into her targeted potential employers.*

• *When finally connecting and meeting with appropriate people in her group of preferred possible employers, she focused on the skills and experiences that she would be bringing to the new opportunity.*

Note: *It took Rachel five weeks from our initial meeting to go through the action steps and land a terrific first job in an organization she had identified and was thrilled to join. She never made a cold call while generating ten relevant initial phone interviews with the twenty-five target companies, five in-person interviews, and three offers. Even as a young, recent college graduate, she was able to network her way to high-value contacts in most of these target organizations*

It was amazing to see the changes in Rachel's confidence level as she developed focus around her unique passions and interests and started to see almost immediate results from her targeted networking.

The most valuable contacts in her clusters turned out to be parents of her college classmates, many of whom either worked with the target companies or knew someone who did. They were happy to help.

Rachel's Targeted Job Search Networking Grid

Music	Animals	Ice Cream	Travel	Fashion
Sony	Bronx Zoo	Hershey	Ritz-Carlton	Coach
Apple	Sea World	Ben and Jerry's	Club Med	Gucci
Carnegie Hall	Seeing Eye Foundation	Haagen-Dazs	Carnival Cruise	Burberry
Broadway Shows	Purina	Bryer's	Irish Tourist	Macy's
Jay Z. and Beyonce	Hartz Mountain	Turkey Hill	Virgin Atlantic	Tiffany's

Any of us can have specific new connections we want to establish for either personal or career objectives. To help guide our search and networking efforts, we need to have our own specific Career Development Action Plan, which we map out in a later chapter.

Chapter Seven

Networking the Room, Even at the White House

Networking the Room, Even at the White House

We all spend large amounts of time at both personal and business events of all kinds. On the personal side, we have weddings, family gatherings, funerals, bar and bat mitzvahs, anniversaries, college reunions, baptisms, cooking classes, birthday celebrations, retirement parties, golf outings, nonprofit and community organization meetings, and many more.

On the business side we have training programs, client presentations, vendor meetings, board meetings, trade shows, career fairs, and industry conferences, for example.

In many respects, all events are the same in that they usually include some people we know well and many people we are meeting for the first time.

So the question comes down to this: How do we maximize the benefits we get from the events we go to. Here are some tips:

• Pick the right events. This seems obvious but it is way too easy to waste time and money going to events that just don't make any sense for you either personally or professionally. Make certain when deciding whether or not to attend an event that the theme of the event is important to you. Make certain the speakers, sponsors, and other attendees are the people with whom you want to meet and start or grow a relationship. It's way too easy to waste precious time and money attending marginal events. This is particularly true these days when we are constantly being bombarded by e-mails inviting us to all kinds of live and web-based events.

• Always bring your business cards with you. I beat this point to death throughout this book. But I cannot emphasize the point strongly enough. Bring enough of them. Why run out?

• Get there early. Thirty minutes or so early to me is the same to me as showing up on time. All of us, regardless of how many events we have attended in our lives, get edgy when we show up at an event where we know few of the people. The more the people participating and the more important the event, the edgier we get. Showing up early, when there may be just a few other early birds standing around, is certainly more comfortable than walking into a packed room with hundreds of people milling around, often already in their own little separate groups talking. Get there early and start talking to others also there ahead of schedule. It will get you in the mood and get your networking juices flowing. Let the event form around you as you move from conversation to conversation. Never show up late after the event is under way. You just give up the opportunity to start creating new relationships in the thirty to forty-five minutes before the events actually start. Why do that?

Showing Up Early at the White House

In early 2013 my partner in our networking coaching firm worked to get us invited to a special meeting at the White House that was organized by Billion + Change, a DC-based group committed to getting corporate America to contribute time and skills to helping nonprofits. The meeting started with a continental breakfast in the White House's Indian Treaty Room at 8:30 a.m.

To gain entrance, we had to pass through a security checkpoint with a street entrance. So we showed up early, by 7:15 a.m., to make certain we beat the crowd and would get a preferred spot during the breakfast portion of the program. A few others also showed up early. While standing waiting for the security checkpoint to open, I started talking with the well-dressed, distinguished-looking gentleman also standing on the sidewalk waiting to enter the White House.

We started talking with me, as usual, doing most of the questioning: "I see you're having Starbucks coffee. Do you enjoy Starbucks? Why are you here? Who are you with? What is your role? What do you hope to learn or accomplish?"

It turned out that my new contact was Herve Humier, president and COO of the Ritz-Carlton hotel company. The company, under Herve's leadership, is highly interested in giving back to inner city young people in the markets having a Ritz-Carlton facility. Because my wife has a nonprofit (Garden State Woman Education Foundation) that focuses on providing college scholarship support and mentoring to inner city New Jersey high school young women, we quickly exchanged business cards and agreed that my new "friend" would connect the person heading the Ritz-Carlton philanthropy work with Judy so they could explore working together.

If I had turned up at the event on time or late, I doubt that conversation would ever have happened. I doubt our paths would even have crossed in the filled rooms where all attendees met.

Also at this event I met Mark Hass, at the time a C-level leader at Edelman, the world's largest PR firm. Mark now heads his own venture investment fund. The time we spent talking at the White House was so productive that we agreed to have a follow-up lunch in New York City. At that discussion I was able to steer the conversation around to Emily Collard, our son Jonathan's girlfriend. Emily was a recent Ohio State graduate, one of Edelman's clients it turned out, and was targeting PR as her career. Mark suggested he bring Emily in for interviews, which she aced. She was hired shortly thereafter and is now, in my view, a rapidly rising star at Edelman.

My networking with Mark did not get Emily this important career opportunity, but it did create the opportunity for Emily to be considered and to sell herself.

• Have your thirty-second profile down pat. Don't fumble your answer when people ask, "What do you do? Why are you here?" Maybe you have to change your profile depending on the nature of the event. You certainly need to have one that is appropriate for that event, that day. Elevator speeches need to be flexible and appropriate for the occasion. One size does not fit all. Don't just wing this. Think about it. Rehearse it before you leave home or your office. Actually, you have way less than thirty seconds to create your first impression, establish your identify and credibility, and motivate the person or people you are talking with to want to know more about you and your organization and to follow up with you. Go with the right mind set, regardless of the type of business or personal event. Go with the expectations that you are going to work hard and smart to meet exceptional new contacts that you can develop after the event. Be positive, be curious, be open, be energetic. Be prepared to share your experiences and unique skills, be prepared to learn about others, and be prepared to find ways to contribute in the future to the others you meet at the event. Be "likeable." Have fun. Start by walking up and talking with people who are standing or sitting by themselves. When networking at events, it can take time to build your momentum, to "get with it." So make it easy to get in the right frame of mind. Find someone standing by themselves, walk over, stick out your hand for a shake, introduce yourself, and start talking. Then repeat the process a few more times before possibly being geared up to approach a group that is already in the middle of their conversations. By getting there early, you often will find an opportunity to meet one or more of the speakers or the people organizing and sponsoring the event. These are likely to be key new connections for you.

• Be willing to get involved in a group discussion that is already under way. After all, others are there for the same reasons you are, to meet new people and learn new things. You may, in fact, turn out to be the most valuable person in the group that has already formed might meet at the event. Be confident in your own identity and networking ability. We all have to develop our own techniques for "breaking in" like this, but I usually just walk up and when there is a lull in the conversation, say, " Hi, I'm Jack Killion. It seems you are having an interesting discussion. Would you mind if I listen in? I am sure I can learn from the group." Of course ninety-nine percent of the time they are going to say yes.

• Develop some "ice breakers" that you can use when meeting new people at an event. There are limitless ways to start a positive conversation with strangers including simply commenting on something that you like about the person: "I like that tie." "Love the color of your dress." "That's an awesome briefcase. Where did you get it?" "I notice you are using an iPad. Do you like it?" Or you can always comment on the event itself: "I have been looking forward to this event. I think the panel discussions will be top notch and well worth attending. What brings you here?" Prepare ahead of time by thinking of the various ways you will feel comfortable breaking the ice, and then use these techniques to begin meeting people and developing the early stages of new relationships.

• Break away from the others from your organization that you came with to the event. Why make the effort to go to an event and then spend all your time talking and sitting with your friends and colleagues who are also attending from your organization? Leave your friends at the registration desk and then spend the rest of the event time on your own, circulating, meeting new people, learning new things.

- I see this "clinging" happen all the time at events. I see it often among young people and women and particularly among "professional" women like CPAs and lawyers. Most men and most women entrepreneurs, "sales types," and C-level executives don't make this mistake. They have enough confidence to fly solo at events. So should you.

- Don't hesitate to break off a discussion with a new contact. Remember, you usually go to an event to meet many new people. So don't get bogged down in any one conversation unless you deem it to be really an important first meeting. It's okay to simply say, "I have enjoyed our conversation and would like to schedule a follow-up phone call or meeting. But, like you, I came here to meet many of the other attendees and participants and need to move on. I have enjoyed our conversation and see synergies between us. I look forward to our next discussion as we agreed." Generally the other person is there for exactly the same reason and thinking exactly the same things, so you are actually doing you both a favor. If you truly believe the new contact belongs in your network, exchange business cards, agree on clear next steps to develop the new relationship, and move on. If you are talking with someone you know is not a fit with you, for whatever reason, simply and politely thank them for taking time to meet. Shake hands, wish him or her good luck at the event, and move on. Don't imply there will be a follow-up action.

- If you are attending an out-of-town event, stay at the hotel suggested by the event organizer. Organizers of events that last more than a day almost always recommend one or more hotels, often where the event is being held. Stay there. That's where you will bump into others attending or leading the event in the elevators, in the coffee shop, at the bar at the end of the day, and in the hospitality suites (if any) that event sponsors host. Keep yourself in the action.

Staying at the Hotel Makes a Difference

For a plastics trade show in Düsseldorf, we had to stay in a hotel 125 miles away.

When I was heading Killion Extruders, the family business that I bought after my dad died, I knew we would have to become an international company if we were to flourish. As an early step in that direction, I decided we would exhibit at the major plastics trade show held in Düsseldorf every few years. It was a major commitment of both time and money to build and ship the equipment we would exhibit, create and ship the exhibit booth itself, and fly and house our team of several people for a week.

I made the rookie mistake of not booking hotel rooms at the same time we committed for the booth space. Money was tight, and I was trying to hold off as long as possible on the hotel down payment to hold the rooms. By the time I did try to book rooms in the city, there were none to be had. Düsseldorf was sold out! The best we could do was to get some single rooms (that two of our team members would have to share) and one double room over 125 miles away by train.

I shared a single room with Don Miller, our VP of international sales and one of my best friends ever. For the week of the show, we alternated nights sleeping either in the bed or in the bathtub!

The Killion team participating in the show spent hours every day commuting by train, always getting there just in time and having to leave the show immediately after the doors closed in order to get back to the small village in which we were staying at a reasonable time. Train service at night was infrequent.

The show was an important success for us despite my fouling up our hotel reservations. However, it could have been so much more if we had been able to stay at any of the Düsseldorf hotels recommended by the show organizer.

- Put in a full day. I see plenty of people attending events on their employer's dime and then putting in a halfhearted appearance, sometimes coming late in the morning after the program is already under way or leaving early to get a round of golf in or maybe do some shopping.

Stick Around

I went to a three-day hedge fund conference in Bermuda recently. By Friday afternoon the crowd was down to just a few of us. I was in Bermuda to meet potential investors as well as to meet and learn about other hedge funds that might be appropriate for our fund's investments in the future.

By the afternoon of the third day (a Friday) at least seventy-five percent of the attendees had left, some leaving for home early or spending the last few hours enjoying Bermuda. During the afternoon break, I was sitting in my row, a couple of chairs down from another person working hard on his laptop. I finally leaned over and introduced myself and asked who he was and why he was still there when most of the others had split.

He said he was the next speaker. He asked me the same thing, why I was still there. I said I was there to listen to the next speaker—him! During that fifteen-minute break, we developed a chemistry based on our common interest in European investing. His fund specialized in investing in emerging Eastern European–based public companies. We agreed to meet a few weeks later in New York City where his US office is located.

His fund is now on our radar screen possibly for a near-term initial investment. If either of us had ducked out of the conference early, that chance meeting and discussion never would have happened.

Networking the Room,
Even at the White House

• Get involved. Don't just attend. When possible, get involved in the event you plan to attend. Offer to talk or participate on a panel if speaking in public is comfortable for you. It should be. Offer to possibly pass along the event information to your database of relevant contacts. Maybe you want to be a sponsor. Often there are sponsorship opportunities for little or no money. What can you barter in exchange for a complimentary sponsorship? Get the list of attendees, sponsors, and exhibitors. Attendee lists are not always available. However, sometimes they are. Even better, try to get the lists of those ahead of time so you can identify and think through how to find and connect with the people of greatest interest for you. When we went to the White House, during President Obama's second term, for a special conference organized by Billion + Change, it was virtually impossible not to meet exceptional people during the several hours we were together for breakfast and the following mini-conference. On the way out, I asked one of the organizers of the event if they had a list of attendees with contact information that I could have. She said of course. What a gold mine that turned out to be.

• If your company is exhibiting, find time to get out of the booth and walk the exhibits in the show. My companies over the years have been exhibitors and presenters at major conferences both in this country and abroad including Russia, Mexico, Venezuela, China, and many countries in Western Europe. Even if short staffed at some of these events, I always found time to "walk the floor" seeing the other exhibits and meeting the other exhibitors. Getting there forty-five minutes before the doors open to nonexhibitors is a high-leverage way to have a few quality conversations with other exhibitors. At most shows at which I have exhibited, one of my objectives is to find possible strategic alliance partners among the other sponsors and exhibitors. It's an important opportunity for this type of networking.

• Plan ahead. I made the point before. If you are going to an event of any type, try to do your homework ahead of time. Know in advance whom you want to meet among other attendees, speakers, exhibitors, or event organizers. Call, e-mail, or message through LinkedIn to the people you are hoping to meet at the events. Schedule your time in advance to maximize your networking efforts.

- Follow up quickly. To repeat another point I emphasize consistently, always follow up quickly with the people you meet and hope to develop a solid relationship with following the event. A quick phone call or e-mail will do wonders to emphasize the seriousness of your interest in building a win-win relationship. Don't just say thanks. Include some indication of what actions you would like to take next, arranging a subsequent meeting, sending information about you, receiving information from them, or setting up a phone call. Be proactive.

Networking at events is one of the techniques most people think about when talking about networking. They often think networking is basically attending a business-oriented event and exchanging business cards. And, voila, good things happen.

Life is not that simple, although networking at events, any type of events, can be a prime way to make many new and significant contacts that convert to results-producing relationships. Events often equal efficient networking. So, besides being alert to the potential opportunities inherent in meeting groups of people at events of all types, make certain you follow the key principles outlined here: do your homework ahead of time, show up early, try to become involved versus just attending, split up from others you come with, stay at a recommended hotel if it is a multiday event, make certain you have your thirty-second profile down pat, bring more than enough business cards, and follow up as agreed with the key people you meet.

Chapter Eight

What? No Place to Network? Create Your Own Networking Event

Besides attending events organized by others, think about organizing your own events. It may sound like a tough thing to do. It is not.

Most of us have experience organizing personal and family events such as surprise parties, class reunions, family reunions, work get-togethers, and the customary birthday and anniversary celebrations.

However, many do not think about organizing events that will benefit their businesses and their careers. For anyone in business, I think developing your own events can be a profit-producing way to market yourself and your business. And it doesn't have to be hard to do. It doesn't take magic to organize and host a successful event. You do not have to hire an event planner to get it done, if you are willing to put the time and effort into making it happen and for the event to be a success.

Ever since I have been on my own developing successful businesses, I have conceptualized and held unique events (I guess at least two hundred) that provided significant benefits and leveraged our marketing dollars. Here are some examples that you might consider or tailor to meet your own needs:

• I went into the magazine business, by being part of the three-man partnership managing Harper's magazine and launching the first national Country Music magazine. We partnered with NYU's Continuing Education Division to organize and host at NYU multiple-day conferences on topics of strong interest to others in the magazine publishing business. Industry experts were happy to talk. We learned from them. Other publications paid to attend. We revenue shared with NYU. We both generated a profit while strengthening our brands, making new connections, and learning from publishing industry experts.

• While breeding, raising, and racing thoroughbred race horses under our Walnut Farm stable brand, I took on a leadership position in the industry. I put together one-day seminars and "experiences" designed to attract new potential owners to the sport. We held Saturday morning seminars at a major New Jersey thoroughbred breeding farm to discuss all the aspects of being an owner. Then we took the attendees in the afternoon to Monmouth Race Track where they could enjoy the experience at the track while being hosted for lunch by prominent jockeys, trainers, and owners. Potential race horse owners paid to spend the day with us. We attracted many new owners into the sport and solidified our Walnut Farm brand as an industry leader.

• When I owned and was heading Killion Extruders, an industrial equipment manufacturing company, we developed a number of different type of events of varying lengths from one to five days:

- Multiday technology conferences held in New Jersey at local hotels and universities. Attendees paid to come to these programs. They paid more than enough to cover our costs. One night during each multiday conference, we would bus the attendees back to our factory for a wine and cheese reception so they could see the equipment we designed and were manufacturing at the time. These were cool events with local musicians providing background music on the factory floor.

-   We held one-day events in US embassies in various parts of the world (UK, Holland, Russia, Mexico, Venezuela, and more). The embassies helped market the events in their host countries and provided the meeting space and food along with simultaneous translators.

-   Doing one-week workshops held at our New Jersey and Florida plants for paying attendees flying up from various Latin American countries, we conducted these in Spanish using several of our Hispanic factory workers as presenters. It gave them a chance to change their routine, get out of their work clothes, see how we dealt with customers, and spend quality time with potential customers. We marketed these events through the plastic industry association in each country and gave the referring association a piece of the revenues generated from their members.

-   We held a morning 5K run through the streets of Chicago during the major international plastic show held every four years at McCormick Place. Participants had to come to our booth to enter the race. We got United Way involved and made a donation to that nonprofit from entry fees we collected. The event generated a lot of positive Chicago and industry press coverage for us including with newspapers and evening TV news. The run brought heavy traffic flow to our booth. Entry fees more than covered our expenses. To run, visitors to the show had to register and get a free Killion Extruders T-shirt at our booth. It was a huge traffic builder for us and created a great deal of goodwill. The run was talked about in the industry for years.

-    I teamed with another ex-McKinsey consultant to launch Wireless for the Corporate User, a multimedia company in the wireless technology space. We developed an ongoing, profitable revenue stream by organizing regional one-day events to educate corporate end users about the wireless and mobile technologies available to them and the benefits they provided.

-    When I started helping my wife with her multimedia Garden State Woman Company, we developed a variety of half- and full-day revenue-producing special events for women including personal financial and health conferences, annual awards luncheons, and networking and relationship development workshops.

-    When I launched my own fund of hedge funds, the Eagle Rock Diversified Fund, it was always in the back of my mind to organize the first-ever hedge fund–focused conference for accredited investors in New Jersey. I still head the successful fund. Finally, in 2012, we held the event, which was a major success from all perspectives with ten hedge funds speaking and over 150 accredited investors attending. The one-day event netted over $30,000 from sponsorship fees paid by the speakers and their hedge funds.

-    When we partnered to launch a training firm to provide executive coaching focused on networking and developing win-win relationships that drive careers and profitable business growth, we started organizing half- and full-day networking sessions for CPAs, our initial target market, which provided CPE credits. We also host half-day networking workshops open to all corporate and professional firm leaders looking to improve their difference-making skills.

I often consult with emerging and leading companies and am always looking for ways for these organizations to develop custom events to build their brand, raise their credibility, leverage their marketing dollars, and generate a new, profitable revenue stream. Opportunities to do this always exist and they always work.

For example, our networking coaching firm recently organized a four-part series of three-hour workshops with a firm of family law attorneys. The partners wanted to get their younger attorneys more engaged in attracting new clients to the firm. At the conclusion of the fourth workshop in the series, we worked with the firm to organize their first annual Education and Networking Event for People in Personal Transition. It was a smashing success and contributed to boosting their brand as the leading family law firm in the region.

The advantages of putting together your own events can be significant. Here are some benefits:

• Invite exactly the people you want to attend and spend time with—in other words, select your current and future potential clients.

• Use the event to generate event profits based on the business model you use for the event. So a marketing effort gets flipped from being an expense to being a profit generator.

• Put together an agenda based on the items you want to learn more about and invite speakers with expertise on those topics. Use events to educate yourself and your organization while generating a few profit dollars.

• Use it to break into new markets including international markets by either putting on unique events in the United States (say in New York City) and/or in other target countries you plan to establish as important markets for your organization. To do this successfully, you generally need to team up with one or more strategic alliance organizations that share your goal of educating and providing value for your target attendees. For example, to organize your own event in New York, assuming you were targeting India and wanted to attract executives from India-based companies, you might approach the New York–based India Chamber of Commerce, the U.S.–India Business Council, or the Sikh American Chamber of Commerce. Or if you wanted to organize an event in one or more key cities in India, you might approach an organization like the Karachi Chamber of Commerce and Industry. Other organizations with which you might partner to develop your own carefully targeted business generating events include leading banks, law firms, and accounting firms.

• In picking partner organizations, you need to think through the benefits to them from working with you and the role you will expect them to play. For example, do you need them to help cover the expenses with sponsors' dollars, market to their database, provide speakers, or be positioned as a co-sponsor to give the event more credibility?

• Increase your visibility, build your brand and credibility, and attract potential new clients.

There are at least three basic business models to use developing your own events.

First, the most expensive format is for you and your organization to absorb all the costs of marketing and hosting the event with both attendees and outside speakers invited to attend with your compliments. I have used this approach when working to penetrate entirely new vertical markets and countries where our company had little exposure and reputation. I used this approach when leading Killion Extruders initial efforts to penetrate markets in other countries. I wanted to make it as easy as possible for target attendees to join us—that is, no cost, feed them, provide lots of top-notch content, and conduct the discussions in their language.

A second option is to charge organizations to be a sponsor, exhibitor, and/or speaker and let attendees come without charge. This works when the theme of the event is designed to introduce and eventually sell high-end services and products to corporate buyers or high-net-worth individuals. You need to be able to deliver the audience that the "sponsors" want to reach.

A word of caution: My experience has been that when participants can sign up to attend an event for free that between twenty and twenty-five percent of those signing up will be "no shows." This is fine as long as you anticipate and plan for this. Of course you still benefit from collecting names of the people who showed interest in what you were doing and, for whatever reason, decided not to attend. Their names become potentially valuable for future marketing efforts.

In the early days of the rollout of wireless and mobile technologies, companies such as AT&T, Ericsson, Motorola, Apple, IBM, the Regional Bell Operating Companies (RBOCs), and others were prepared to pay to have their capabilities presented to two hundred to seven hundred potential customers attending half-day and full-day wireless briefings we organized for corporate buyers. The audience size depended on the location. New York drew the most. Surprisingly Dallas was the second best market for these types of events. We also ran a two-day combination conference and exhibition in Boston that focused exclusively on the use of these new communications technologies in the health care sector.

This model also works when the target audience consists of consumers unable to pass through an attendance fee on their expense accounts. Most consumers these days are cautious and don't like spending their own money to attend events. So the paying speakers and sponsors have to be ones that target the consumer market—for example, financial planners, unique health care providers, specialty retailers, insurance providers, private schools, and others.

A third option is to charge the attendees and get the leading speakers without paying speakers fees. I have always been successful getting leading experts to talk in exchange simply for the exposure they get. I have charged attendees as much as $3,500 and attracted nearly three hundred for a two-day event when the topic was of vital importance to the attendees and when the speakers were top drawer enough. This model works when the attendees' employer organizations will pick up the expenses to travel and attend and you deliver the presenters that attendees need to hear.

Complimentary and paid webcasts are another option for hosting your own events. In this challenging economy, organizations are reluctant to pick up the tab for employees to travel and stay overnight at out-of-town events. In some circumstances, webcasts help fill a need for companies to pull an audience together. But recognize that these Internet-based events will not take the place of the belly-to-belly networking and relationship development that takes place at live events.

Keys to Successfully Organizing Your Own Events

Plenty of books have been written on event planning, so no need to go into depth here. But just to get you thinking, here are a few points to pay attention to:

• Almost anyone with average abilities can plan and organize a successful event. It's not rocket science. Don't be afraid to think it through. If you believe you have a good idea, go ahead and give it a shot.

• Have a plan and budget for the event. It need not be complicated. Your plan should include attention to these details:

- Your objectives, which could include generating a profit from the event, elevating your brand in the target market, and developing important new contacts. Be clear and be specific so you and your team understand the goals and can do a thorough job after the event assessing the effort and identifying ways to make it better next time.

- Your financial expectations including revenues generated and itemized estimates of various expenses to be incurred.

- The venue where the event will be hosted. This is really important. It has to be conveniently located to your target attendees. It needs to be the right type of facility for the type of event you are planning. The "deal" you can arrange for the facility is obviously important. I have found every venue is open to negotiate terms rather than lose the business. For example, I have never paid a room rental fee. In general, for half- or full-day events, I find it difficult to attract people from farther away than twenty or so miles from the event location. So try to plop your event right in the middle of a dense population of your target attendees. My successful exception to this distance challenge was when I organized high-value, multiday events in New Jersey for Latin American attendees from the plastic industry. If your agenda and event content is important enough, people will come.

- The event agenda and logistics for the day. Deciding foods to be provided can be an important and often overlooked key point. The most unsuccessful event I ever attended flopped because the organizers badly underestimated the number of attendees. They attracted many more walk-ins than expected and under ordered the food required for lunch. It was not a pretty scene!

- Your marketing plan for getting speakers, sponsors, and attendees. Do you need an event website? Will you use PR and Constant Contact or Mail Chimp messaging? Do you need incentives to attract attendees? For example, for events involving an attendance fee, it has always worked for me to offer discounts to multiple people coming from the same organization when they register together.

- Staffing the event and providing the handout materials.

- Getting feedback from the event so next year's can be better.

Always start out assuming and branding your events as annual events. If it deserves to be done once, it will deserve to be done annually.

- The post-event follow-up to sponsors and attendees, where you get bang for your buck. Get back to both quickly to say thanks and to get their written evaluations. Comments in these evaluations can be especially important content for next year's marketing materials for the follow-up program. Very few things beat the credibility power of strong testimonials from previous event attendees.

• Start with the theme of the event. Make it compelling to both speakers and attendees. It's hard to imagine any topic that could not be turned into a "successful" event—such as trout fishing, cosmetic surgery, growing tomatoes, stock market investing, launching your own business, and hundreds of other ideas.

• Get out a yellow pad and start planning the agenda in fifteen-minute bites regardless of the length of the event. If you cannot develop a detailed specific agenda at the very outset, you have little shot of pulling the event off successfully.

• Decide the business model you will use. Who pays the freight and will the event generate a profit plus accomplish the other goals you have?

• Give yourself enough time to pull it together. I normally like to have three months or sometimes a little longer to plan and organize every aspect of my events including date(s), time of the event, location, target speakers, target attendees, marketing pieces, and food and beverages. If you have never put together a fairly substantial event, give yourself five to six months to pull it all together.

• While you may need months to organize a major event, I generally think three to four weeks' lead notice is sufficient to announce and get the one-day event on your target attendees' schedules. Events lasting several days need a longer lead time to attract attendees.

• Pick the right location for the event, which takes into account several factors including access, costs, parking, available technology, quality of the venue, and whether or not the facility matches the theme. People have to be able to get there. I held one event in LA, never again. Traffic there is so bad that people had real trouble getting to the conference site on time. Most of those who did show up in the morning left early to battle the late afternoon traffic. At the end of the day in a breakout room, we only had three people, the speaker/sponsor, me, and one listener who got up and left early. We refunded the sponsorship fee obviously.

• Can you attract the attendees and the speakers/sponsors? Do you have the necessary clout in the marketplace and will the event provide compelling benefits to all the participants? Are your theme and speakers prominent enough to be a draw?

• Give responsibility for pulling the event together successfully to someone capable of thinking and acting like an entrepreneur. Maybe that is you. Maybe it is someone else on your team.

• Track progress frequently, a short meeting once a week usually is frequent enough until you get within three to four weeks of the actual event date. Then you may want to check on progress daily or every couple of days.

I have found over the past forty years that organizing my own profit-producing events, regardless of the industry I was working in at the time, was one of the single best ways to build our brand, expand my network of important connections, initiate long-term win-win relationships, and boost sales and leverage marketing dollars.

I love the concept of generating a profitable revenue stream by having clients and potential clients come to us versus us having to send salespeople to their locations. This concept is one that most organizations fail to capitalize on.

Chapter Nine

What Do Boy Scouts, Girl Scouts, and Little League Have in Common?

Joining Existing Groups

E arly in my career, there were few groups to join that offered networking opportunities and other benefits, but there were some.

For young kids, there were the Brownies, Cubs, Boys Scouts and Girl Scouts, Little League and others. All could be considered viable networking groups designed to bring young like-minded kids together for learning, team building, and camaraderie. For adults there were community groups such as Kiwanis, Rotary, the Lions, chambers of commerce, and the Zonta Club for women.

In 1950 a young corporate president saw the value in bringing together other young corporate presidents in a group he called the Young Presidents' Organization (YPO) that today has over twenty thousand members in over 120 countries. They claim "YPO is the most powerful network in the world for business leaders." What a great brand that is!

Based on a good friend's several-decade-long membership in YPO and in the successor organization they created for executives who reached the aging-out point in YPO, I realize what a powerful resource this group has been and continues to be for its members.

Today, everything is different. Networking is a hot topic. Belonging to various special-interest networking groups is a growing trend with an almost limitless range of options to consider—for example, these:

• Women can join various executive women's groups. I question, however, how helpful belonging exclusively to all-women's networking groups can be helping women, particularly younger ones, break into the "good old boy" network that dominates many organizations. Why not join and become active in a targeted group or two that includes both women and men?

• Recent college graduates can join their alumni and young professionals' industry or regional groups.

• The civic minded among us can join service clubs such as Rotary and Kiwanis and various local, national, or international nonprofits' boards of directors.

• Working professionals can join groups organized for their industry or just for networking in their communities. BNI and LeTip are two such global networking organizations with local branches or chapters.

• The rest of us can join groups organized around interests, for example, bird-watching, butterfly and wine clubs, reading clubs, cigar clubs, motorcycle clubs, language clubs, cooking clubs, golf, swimming, fishing, knitting, and tennis and more.

The range of opportunities to network within groups is almost limitless. And if you don't find one that exactly fits your networking goals, you can always think about launching your own group.

Keys to Successfully Networking in Groups

Pick the right group in the first place. This may seem obvious, but sometimes it takes investing some time and money by participating in a group before discovering there is or is not a fit for you. Here's a hint: when considering joining a networking group, it's not the number of participants that is important. Far more important is who the members are and if there is open, honest, consistent, and constructive communication going on, both at and in between group meetings.

Richard Shapiro, a good friend, author of The Welcomer Edge: Unlocking the Secrets to Repeat Business and who also provided a testimonial for this book, recently spoke to me about the importance of spending quality networking time with the right people. It had been his personal experience that, while he was an effective networker (I know this to be true), he concluded he could do a better job of picking the people with whom he networked. As a result of realizing this, he is now targeting his networking contacts and recently became a member of two groups that fit his business objectives closely. They are the Luxury Marketing Council in New York and Execs in the Know.

When joining a group, your objective should be to stay with it long term since there is evidence that the longer a person belongs and is active in a group, the more likely he or she annually will get more and higher value referrals.

In his book The World's Best Known Marketing Secret, founder and chief visionary officer of BNI Ivan Misner writes about the value of referrals and number of referrals being linked directly to length of membership in a group. He makes the point that, in a study he conducted, members for one or two years identified their largest referral to be more than fifty times higher than it was for members for less than a year.

It may take time to find the groups to join—the number is

almost limitless both in person and online. But consider these issues when evaluating joining any particular groups:

• Your dollar investment to belong.

• Frequency of meetings. If you join you should plan to attend all or nearly all of their meetings. Will your schedule allow that?

• Location of meetings. Can you get there?

• Timing of meetings. Will your family and professional commitments accommodate the group's meeting schedule?

• Membership. Are all or most of the members people with whom you will value building relationships? How many members are involved? I think a group of twenty to twenty-five is more than enough to yield real advantages.

• Opportunities for you to be a leader. In group situations leaders always seem to reap the most benefits.

• Are you comfortable with the structure and bylaws of the group?

• Focus. Is the main focus of the group consistent with the things that interest you the most and about which you are the most passionate? Are the members potentially great contacts?

• Will participating provide you with a strong enough R.O.T.—Return on your Time?

Over the years I have checked out several and joined a few networking groups that for a variety of reasons did not work out for me after being initially attractive.

For example, I attended two BNI meetings as a guest of a

What Do Boy Scouts, Girl Scouts,
and Little League Have in Commmon?

member and found their highly structured format with early-morning weekly meetings and a commitment to produce at least a set number of referrals a week did not fit my style and business objectives. BNI did not work for me and my approach and goals for networking. However, it works quite well for other business leaders, particularly those with a relatively tight geographical new business development focus and for those targeting small business owners and middle managers in larger organizations.

Charlie Lawson, Co-National Director of BNI in the UK and Ireland, made the point that the average businessperson has a thousand contacts, and if you are in a group networking with forty other business leaders, you could have access to forty thousand possible connections. "That's when networking gets interesting," he said.

I went to one LeTip International meetings and didn't find their localized, small business membership helpful. But for others, LeTip obviously works. On their website, they position themselves as "LeTip International, the world's largest, privately owned, professional business leads organization. Since 1978, LeTip programs have helped over 120,000 members, throughout the United States and Canada, build business success through personal referrals."

The Gotham Group Is a Powerful Networking Organization

I have been a member of a chapter of Gotham, an exceptional networking group. This chapter and group meets my business development needs very well. Chapter members are all senior leaders of major corporations or they own their own substantial businesses. Meetings are monthly with most being held in the city at the end of the day.

Two good friends, employment attorneys Fred Klein and Nancy Schess, have done an amazing job over more than a decade of building their networking-focused Gotham Group (Gothamnetworking.com). One goal when they launched the group was to drive revenues for their law firm, Klein, Zelman, Rothermel, Jacobs & Schess.

Over the years, however, Gotham has taken on a life of its own that now includes specific sub-Gotham groups in multiple locations, most in the metro New York region. Gotham groups are formed around specific professional interests, careers, and lifestyles. Each group decides how their Gotham Group will operate under the overall Gotham umbrella.

A portion of all Gotham Clubs' dues are funneled back to the mother ship and are used to organize events like golf outings that are open to members of all Gotham groups, develop and host the Gotham website, and manage Fred's List, an e-mail announcement blast that gets circulated daily to members about connections Gotham members are seeking both personally and professionally. Some of the relationships and benefits that have come out of the Fred's List service have been both lifesaving and career and business building.

Try to attend a few meetings of whatever group you consider before committing to be a member. It will also be useful to meet with some of the group's members outside the group meeting itself. Letting you "kick the tires" will be in the best interest of everybody. Groups are not looking to recruit inappropriate new members. Groups want to make certain there is a fit as well.

Create Your Own Networking Groups

Rather than joining other already existing networking-oriented groups, give some thought to starting your own group. I have done this several times and expect to do it several more times in the future. Here to spark your creativity are some example groups I created as well as a couple of networking-focused groups created by others:

• Several years ago, when our son, Jonathan, was entering his fourth

176

What Do Boy Scouts, Girl Scouts, and Little League Have in Commmon?

year at Georgetown University, he decided to put together a group of three personal advisors to help him land his first career opportunity out of college. I was one of the chosen ones along with an investment bank friend of his plus the former head of direct marketing globally for Time Warner. The role of the advisory group was to help him with his resume, provide relevant new contacts and introductions, and help prep him for interviews. Nearly all of the communication was via phone and e-mails. The three advisors all knew each other and were able easily to share their thinking with each other and with Jonathan. More college students should think about using this technique to help propel their early career moves. It is an example of putting together a personal networking group with a specific purpose and for a specific length of time.

After Jonathan graduated, we teamed up to put together a "life team" to help guide him in the future. On the team he had a lawyer, an accountant, an insurance provider, and a wealth advisor. Jonathan interviewed two of each before making his decision which ones to include on his team. His argument to a highly talented group of professionals was compelling. In the early years, when his career was just launching, his earnings would be modest and complications in his life likely to be minimal. He would not require much of their time, and fees he paid to them would be modest.

As his career developed and his earnings and assets grew along with potential life complications, he would likely need more of their time and expertise. At that point he would be positioned to pay for their greater input. As he developed successful experiences working with his team, he would be sharing these with his quality friends from college, all with high-potential careers. In essence he would become a farm system for creating other potential young clients for his "life team" advisors.

Plus Jonathan was the glue that helped bind these professionals together in the new relationships they created by working with Jonathan.

This type of ongoing networking group has the potential to

be a years- or decades-long powerful personal resource. More people should consider developing their own "life team" and ones for their kids as they start their careers.

• A couple of years ago, I was asked by MIT to organize a networking group in New Jersey for graduates of the MIT Sloan Business School. I thought this would be an amazing group to bring together and would create all types of important win-win relationships for me and the other participants. After a false start or two, we now have a group going smoothly. We are building strong friendships that often include our families. We are finding ways to "partner" from both a business and personal point of view, and we are sharing unique resources that many of us have individually and that are now being made available to the group. We meet about every six weeks with a break for the winter. The format is basically an open discussion held during a Dutch-treat dinner and drinks.

• I mentioned I head a fund of hedge funds, the Eagle Rock Diversified Fund. We are invested in a New York–based hedge fund that primarily invests in corporate and sovereign debt in emerging countries including those in Latin America, Africa, Asia, and the Middle East. The head of the hedge fund, a good friend, is one of the few people I know who can put all the pieces together globally. Because he and his team invest so broadly geographically, he understands the opportunities and challenges on a worldwide basis.

One day I told him I didn't know many people of his caliber with the same depth of international expertise and knowledge, but that I knew a few. I suggested I invite some of my contacts to come together in his conference room one afternoon after the market closed to just meet and talk, no agenda other than exchanging business cards and ideas. The group that showed up was amazing and included one of the leaders of the Rockefeller Group, the corporate counsel of Avon, an exec of a Fortune 500 women's product company dependent on emerging markets for almost all their growth, the head of a New

What Do Boy Scouts, Girl Scouts, and Little League Have in Commmon?

York–based marketing firm serving the US financial services sector and representing countries wanting to reach this market, a lawyer specializing in tech transfer with European universities wanting to bring their developments to the United States, and an investment banking friend who worked with Michael Eisner bringing the Disneyland project to fruition in Europe and then headed M&A for US Surgical, a medical device company making strategic acquisitions in Europe.

The initial meeting was so successful that we agreed to continue meeting on a loose once-a-quarter schedule, each time at a different participant's office.

- In 2014 I met Roger Barton, a New York lawyer heading his own firm. I was impressed. We hit it off immediately. I realized Roger also had a network of exceptional people. So, at the end of our first meeting, I suggested we each invite ten of our special connections to spend two hours of late afternoon time networking in Roger's conference room to meet new, interesting, accomplished people and enjoy some fruit, coffee, and cookies. To avoid possible duplications, Roger reviewed my list of targeted invitees, and I reviewed his. Before the get-together we had everybody send me 125 words describing their business backgrounds and providing their contact data. I collected these in a handout that I e-mailed to everyone ahead of time plus handed out a hard copy at the start of our time together.

We made it clear to everyone that we were not launching a new networking group. There are enough of those already in the metro NY area. This would be a one-time only meeting of interesting successful people that Roger and I thought each attendee would be interested in meeting. Of course the meeting went well past the planned two-hour time limit, and many new and important relationships started to form that day.

- Three New York–based organizations teamed to form a group to be coached by our networking coaching firm over a several month span.

A leading bank, accounting firm, and law firm each agreed to split our fees three ways and have each send ten of their highest potential senior staff members to attend the four three-hour networking and relationship development workshops that we organized with a month in between each session. The conference room locations of the workshop rotated among the three participating firms.

Besides learning to sharpen their networking and relationship building skills by coming together in this unique group, the participants also had twelve hours to develop new relationships with the twenty members of the other two organizations. Plus, they deepened their relationships with the other nine workshop participants from their own firm—in other words, they were networking both externally and internally!

At the conclusion of the fourth and final workshop, each participant was asked to invite at least one relevant guest to attend a ninety-minute "networking" event held at the accounting firm. Our firm provided a twenty-minute keynote speaker to open the event that gave the workshop participants the opportunity to use their newly enhanced networking and relationship development skills to trigger new business relationships with the guests.

• In late 2014, a senior level, engagement manager participant in another networking coaching program we organized for a top three accounting firm, described the difficulty all senior members of the firm had becoming partners. He estimated he was five to six years away from partnership consideration. To make this huge leap, it was extremely important that he demonstrate in the next several years a real ability to drive the revenue growth of the firm. Their ideal new client generates $500,000 or more in annual fees. He asked for our thoughts.

Since he was a Lehigh University finance graduate, we suggested that we help him form his own networking group consisting of fifteen to twenty other Lehigh finance graduates. The qualifications of those invited to participate included the following:

What Do Boy Scouts, Girl Scouts, and Little League Have in Commmon?

- Graduated within ten years of his graduation date on the older side and within three years of his graduation on the more recent side. For example, assuming he graduated in 2005 and was thirty-one, he would invite other Lehigh finance majors to join his networking group who graduated between 1995 and 2008. Their ages would range from about twenty-eight to forty-one.

- Had to be working in New Jersey in a financial management position with a Fortune 500 corporation with which they had spent at least the past five years. Only one participant per corporation would be included in the new group and clearly had to embrace the mission and ground rules of this newly formed group, which was to foster developing win-win relationship among like-minded rising financial executives committed to sharing their experiences, guidance, and connections within the networking group. The common denominators among all the participants were these: Lehigh financial educations, age range and senior level, successful employment track record with a major international corporation.

Our young client went ahead with this concept and created his own networking group as his own unique "farm system" for growing his own future client base among major international corporations. The theory was, as his members advance within their corporations or within other corporations they might join in the future, some of them would be the decision-makers deciding where their audits, taxes, and other key accounting work would be done. Given his leadership role in putting together this networking group of major corporate financial executives, he should be in a prime position to land a great deal of these assignments.

Late in 2015 as this book is going to press, the monthly dinner group meetings with nineteen participants are going well, and the founder is having "the time of his life" spending quality time with his peers.

Other similarly positioned accountants in his firm are now thinking of creating their own similar networking groups, and his internal reputation is developing as a "difference maker."

This is obviously a business development model, based on networking and relationship development that can be used by professionals in a range of organizations from law firms to banks to investment and insurance firms plus other accounting organizations.

I am now thinking through creating my own networking group in New Jersey. The working title is Jack's Group. I just think there will be so much value in bringing together ten or twelve connected, successful people, all of whom I think should know and be working with each other. I will cherry-pick the members of the group. The concept is that the group would be together for a year with six meetings during the year, more than enough time for everyone to get to know each other and make a determination if and how they can work together going forward. At the end of the year, we will close down this group and maybe start another one for year two with ten or twelve entirely different members.

The reasons for starting your own networking group or groups must be obvious and may include these ideas:

• Start it for whatever personal or professional purpose you want to pursue. You decide the mission.

• Invite whomever you want to participate. You control the membership. You are the gatekeeper.

• Structure it anyway you want from casual and informal to quite formal. I personally like to keep things flexible, so in most of the groups I put together, we don't have dues or an official structure with officers and bylaws. For our MIT Sloan alumni group, for example, we hold our meetings from six to about nine in the evening with a pay-your-own dinner approach to cover the costs of food and drinks.

What Do Boy Scouts, Girl Scouts, and Little League Have in Commmon?

- Meet as frequently or infrequently as you think best for your purposes. You get to pick the location and timing of the meetings—such as mornings, lunchtime, evenings, weekdays, or weekends.

Consider some of these issues when deciding to become your own networking group organizer:

- It will take some of your time to launch the group and keep it going. Are you willing to make the time commitment? You will be surprised, however, at how little time it actually does take once you have the first couple of meetings under your belt.

- Can you attract the right types of people to join and stick with the group? Everybody these days is super busy. Are you a big enough draw or is your basic idea powerful enough? Will participants see real value for themselves in getting involved?

- Do you have access to the target members? In the case of the MIT Sloan alumni networking group I put together, I would not have been able to pull this off without having access to MIT's database of New Jersey Sloan graduates. In most cases putting together the group that you want and that will succeed will come down to whether or not you have the right people in your network already or if you have access to them.

- What happens if you start and the effort fails? You never want to be viewed as someone who starts but can't successfully complete projects. Organizing your own captive group can enhance or hurt your reputation and personal brand. Don't go down this path unless you are committed and convinced you can and want to make it work.

People like working with and spending time with leaders with exceptional personal and professional brands. Being recognized as the one who successfully pulled together a cohesive group of people committed to being resources for each other can clearly be an important step in developing your own unique brand.

Chapter Ten

How You Are Perceived Is Key: Be Smart Creating and Managing Your Personal Brand

We are all a brand. Noted author Tom Peters coined the phrase "Brand You" in his book by the same name. It's a worthwhile read.

Our personal brand can either work for us or against us. Planned or unplanned, we create our own unique brand in a variety of ways.

How we dress is part of our brand. Johnny Cash wore black. That was part of his brand. Larry King wears suspenders. They are part of his brand. Madonna wears outrageous outfits on stage. That is part of her brand. Lady Gaga blows us away with her far-out outfits, all part of her brand. The point is how you dress characterizes you and contributes to your brand. Are you dressing the way you want to be perceived?

Your physical appearance is part of your brand. To some extent we can't totally control parts of our appearance, but we can control aspects of it. Are you fit or heavy and out of shape? Do you keep your hair the way you want to look? When I was in the country music industry, I spent many hours with one of the greatest country music performers of all times. Now in his late seventies, he is still performing today. When we first met, I quickly noticed that he worked hard to keep his hands out of sight. They might be in his pockets or under his folded arms. When I finally did see his hands, I realized what he didn't want people to see. His fingers were badly nicotine stained and his nails severely bitten down. To this day I remember how uncomfortable we both were when we met and he so deliberately made sure his hands were not visible. Unattractive hands were part of his brand and a part that I am sure he wished had been different.

Your vocabulary is part of your brand. Your tone and actual language helps shape your brand. Is there anything worse than someone who curses inappropriately or tell off-color jokes? I always wince, at least a little, when someone uses the F word in a discussion, even if it's just boys being boys.

Your friends are part of your brand. Do you spend time with winners or losers? Soaring with the eagles is where you need to be.

Your accomplishments are part of your brand. Your education and work experiences contribute big-time to your professional brand. Often these are the first things people see about you when you apply for a new position, or a bank loan or when you are being considered for an important membership or maybe a board position.

As an educational counselor, I have been interviewing high school kids applying to MIT for nearly twenty years. I typically interview fifteen to twenty young people a year. Even at that young age, their accomplishments become part of their brand and play a major role in the conclusions I reach about them. Further along in your life and your career, your most recent accomplishments become the important ones that people consider in their evaluation of you. But a strong educational background will always help you carry a positive personal brand.

Over the years of hiring many people for various types of businesses, I have found three cases of people falsifying their backgrounds. These surfaced after I had already hired them and was disappointed in their performances. So I went back to check. In one case, a candidate I had hired in a marketing role claimed earning an MBA from a local college. That never happened. I hired another person in an important sales role based on his sister-in-law's recommendation. I thought I knew her well and valued her recommendation. He claimed a college degree from the University of New Hampshire. It turned out the school had never heard of him let alone granted him a degree. Another I hired for an engineering role listed working for one of our major competitors for several years in a similar position to the one we recruited him to fill. Turned out he had never worked for the other company.

People falsifying information on their resumes and on their LinkedIn profiles happens all the time. The undercoverrecruiter.com reports that forty-six percent of resumes for job applications contain false information with twenty-one percent including fraudulent degrees in their backgrounds. Padding resumes is not smart! And lying does not speak well for your character.

Your personal and family lifestyles are part of your brand. How your kids develop, where and how you live, how you spend your "free" time, the type of car you drive, how well you manage your personal finances and take care of your home and property, whether you get involved in the community and take on leadership roles all speak volumes about you.

Your education as well as your personal and business accomplishments are part of your brand. Do you have a solid education and a proven career track record? Are you involved in your community in a meaningful way? What have you done in your personal life that sets you apart?

The exposure you generate for yourself is part of your brand. If expanding your exposure is important to you, then find ways to possibly author articles or blogs in your areas of interest. Or be invited to speak in front of groups with which you are interested in working.

Being published in various blogs and magazines such as Citi's small business blog, the New York Law Journal and the New York Enterprise Report obviously benefits me and elevates my brand.

My opinion on the best way to get published is simply to pick out the publication you want to write for, understand their audience and the types of articles they publish, and then write what you believe will be appropriate. E-mail your content to the editor with a note that you think the attached material fits their editorial mission. Generally, editors are always looking for new sources and fresh thinking. If you have been smart picking your target publication and writing a well-done, relevant article, then, chances are, it will get published. This is far better than sending a note to the editor asking if they could use an article that you would like to write for them. Those types of inquiries usually wind up in the trash, typically without being acknowledged.

I have many speaking opportunities offered to me. They all come from people in my network who know groups looking for speakers. If speaking appeals to you as a way to share your knowledge and help develop your brand, start letting people in your network know that you are looking for opportunities. A caution, make certain you feel comfortable talking in public and have the ability to excite and inform the people you want to reach and influence.

And, of course, pay real attention to the brand you create on the Internet with your Facebook and LinkedIn and other social media platforms. Today, even before people meet with you, they will check you out online either by Googling you or looking for your LinkedIn profile. I am astounded at how poorly many professionals and business leaders do with their LinkedIn profiles. Many have just a relatively few connections. Too many lack a photograph, which just raises a huge red flag. Many others don't keep their online profile current, and some even have their previous employer still listed as where they currently work.

How You Are Perceived is Key:
Be Smart Creating and Managing Your
Personal Brand

A Leader at the UN Found Me on LinkedIn

One day, out of the blue, I was contacted on LinkedIn by someone with the United Nations asking to be connected with me. I was skeptical, wouldn't you be? But after reviewing his profile, I agreed to connect and sent a message suggesting we have coffee one day in the city on one of my upcoming trips to New York. Instead of coffee, my new connection subsequently invited me to have lunch at the UN in the delegates' dining room.

Turned out my new contact has responsibility through his role at the UN for combating international terrorism and human rights violations. He believes that empowering women and creating entrepreneurs in emerging countries are two important tools to use to combat these atrocities. He was interested in the information in my LinkedIn profile describing my involvement with Judy's Garden State Woman Education Foundation that clearly is empowering women of all ages and in all circumstances. He was also interested in my forty years of developing new ventures and teaching entrepreneurial skills.

I would love to work with my new friend at the UN and find ways to contribute to these two global challenges. We have held several meetings to discuss how to make this happen. Hopefully we will find the right model for working together.

Not Paying Attention to His LinkedIn Profile

A one-on-one coaching client was having trouble developing business after the midsize agency he had been with was acquired by a top-ten global insurance firm. With his three-year employment agreement nearing an end, he was advised to hire me as a business development coach. Very quickly his inexperience and lack of skills as an effective

189

networker surfaced. I could write books about his challenges including a weak LinkedIn profile.

As we went through his profile, we spent some time talking about his college experience in which he only listed the dates and degree he received attending a midsize New England university. With prodding, he mentioned he had played football all four years, made all-conference the last two years, and was elected captain of the team as a senior. He agreed including this information would have added to his personal brand as a competitive leader and team player.

His profile was so weak and he was apparently bright, so I asked why his LinkedIn presence was inadequate. He indicated he had let his administrative assistant write and post his profile without any real input from him. He didn't think it justified his spending time on it. Obviously this was an ill-informed decision.

The point is, your web presence is important, particularly your use of LinkedIn from a business perspective. Develop and maintain your profile wisely.

In an article titled, "How Social Networks Network Best," MIT Professor Alex Pentland makes the point that employees in one organization he researched with the most extensive personal digital networks were seven percent more productive. However, employees in the same organization with the most cohesive face-to-face networks were thirty percent more productive.

Belly-to-belly networking is still where you will get the most bang for your buck!

Chapter Eleven

Your Culture at Home and Work Is Critical. It's Amazing What You Can Accomplish over Eggs

Your family's culture and the culture of the organization you work with both impact your ability and motivation to network successfully.

For sure, families have their own cultures. The degrees of trust and flexibility that exist in a family can vary greatly. Parents can be more or less flexible with their expectations of each other and of their kids.

Culture at Home

On the personal side, networking of any kind, either personal or business related, takes time that could otherwise be spent with the family. Spouses can react differently to this challenge. I have been involved in several partnerships formed to launch new businesses or buy and grow existing ones. In one partnership, my partner had a wife who kept a tight leash on him, frequently calling toward the end of the day to see when he would be home.

Working on a weekend, particularly if it involved "networking," almost always caused issues for my partner, which, in turn, put real pressures on our partnership. Eventually the pressures of trying to launch a new business got to my partner. One day he simply announced he was leaving the partnership and walked away to take a paid position with a midsized corporation outside the financial sector.

The culture within his second family—he had been married before—did not support the intense entrepreneurial effort required from both of us to help grow our new business, which included extensive networking. We jointly agreed a more conventional nine-to-five, middle-management career working with a privately owned company was a better fit given his family culture.

I have never run into this type of issue or pressure at home. Judy and our son, Jonathan, always realized that for me to develop a meaningful career or grow a business that benefits us all, I have to be out doing things at various times. I also realized that for Judy to continue to grow her Garden State Woman Education Foundation, she too has to be out of the house and out of her office meeting people, developing solid, long-term win-win relationships. It's just one of the facts of life for almost anyone trying to develop a successful career. Being successful both personally and professionally is not a nine-to-five, five-days-a-week proposition.

I wrote earlier that I found one way to foster a networking friendly culture at home is frequently to involve Judy and Jonathan in some of my networking efforts, particularly discussions conducted over breakfast, at night, or on the weekend and involving having coffee or a meal. I am a big believer in starting most days off, usually at a local diner, with a meeting over coffee and eggs.

I have very few meetings of this type that would be awkward having either or both Judy and Jonathan sitting in for at least part of the discussion. Other times they come with me, get introduced to the person I am meeting, but then sit elsewhere in the diner or restaurant doing their own thing. For readers with younger kids, this approach to networking can be an exceptional and easy way to help teach their kids about the business world. I don't think it is ever too early to start their learning curve.

This approach is not one way. When I am meeting people at a typical family time, for example, on a weekend, and I know the discussion will not be sensitive in any way, I often suggest he or she bring the family. Often this happens.

Several years ago I served for three years on the board of directors of a public UK company, the one that bought Killion Extruders. Generally I took both Judy and Jonathan to the UK when I traveled for board meetings. Over time, the other board members got to meet, know, and develop friendships with both Judy and Jonathan. Several invited the three of us to have lunch or dinner with them and their families. This was a seamless way to make certain my family felt involved in what I was doing career-wise. It also was a good way for board members and company leaders to get a better feel for me as a person.

The point is Judy and Jonathan know generally they are welcome to come along to many of my networking meetings. The reverse is also true. Sometimes they invite me to tag along to their meetings. It makes it easy for all of us to feel involved in what we are all doing. Just recently the firm that Jonathan works for, Carl Marks Advisors, invited clients and friends of the firm to spend a day in a private box watching a New York Mets game. I was invited to join the twenty-five others who would be attending. I got to meet some of the other key leaders at the firm plus some of Jonathan's clients and strategic alliances. I made some contacts that I am sure will be important in the future to my career and personally.

The point is this: be aware that the important family culture will impact your ability to network successfully. Be creative about sharing many of these opportunities and experiences. I think the more you can involve each other in these activities, the better.

Culture in the Business World

The 2015 CEO survey conducted by the Conference Board identified solving the puzzle of creating an innovative culture that spurs increased workforce productivity as being one of the key issues challenging CEOs. An organization with a high-impact, winning culture will have five key elements all hitting on all four cylinders:

• Leadership will be strong, fair, skilled, trusted, respected, and empowering.

• Members will be strongly engaged with the organization's mission, leaders, products, services, and programs.

• Members will have strong relationships with each other. They have friends at work.

• The atmosphere will be positive and upbeat. People will believe they are treated fairly and that they are appreciated and valued. Clearly it will be a fun, exciting place to work. When evaluating businesses for whatever reason, I immediately get a sense of the atmosphere when I walk in. Are people smiling and talking? Are they walking quickly? Is there high energy? Are they brainstorming in groups? Atmosphere matters.

• Innovation is happening. To innovate new products and services, people need to work together effectively in teams and they need uninterrupted "think" time.

If you agree with this assessment of key elements in a winning environment, then you will also agree that networking and developing relationships are critical skills needed to help drive the development of a powerful and positive culture.

Too many organizations (maybe most) lack a culture that truly supports, encourages, and benefits from effective results-producing networking. They badly underestimate the potential power of effective internal networking on the performance of the organization.

Networking skills are seldom considered or emphasized when making hiring decisions. Nor are they typically part of formal performance evaluations. Networking training is almost never provided. Employees hesitate frequently to be out of the office "networking." Too often, when they do network, they are reluctant to turn in networking-incurred expenses, although their efforts were clearly aimed at helping the company grow.

Too often, people are trapped in non-supportive silo cultures. I see this problem in all types and sizes of organizations including law, accounting, consulting and other professional firms, colleges and universities, government agencies, charities, and corporations.

Siloed law enforcement units, instead of networking and cooperating, frequently squabble over who controls and gets credit for successful major investigations.

In June 2015 two convicts, with life sentences for murder, broke out of the maximum security prison in Dannemora in upstate New York with help from a prison correction staff member. How corrupt must the culture of Dannemora be?

The New York Post in its June 15, 2015 edition, in the Inside Albany column authored by Fredric U. Dicker, wrote about the silos at work impeding efforts to apprehend the two escapees: "The massive manhunt for two escaped murderers from the Dannemora prison has been hampered by state police secrecy, interagency rivalries, and the disruptive involvement of Governor Cuomo." He went on, "The state police are trying to make certain they're the ones to catch these guys, and that they get all the credit, and as a result, they are not making full use of the assets that are available to them." Further, "The state police, the lead agency, had repeatedly refused to share information on the design and scope of the manhunt with the local police, the Clinton County Environmental Conservation Department whose police officers are part of the search, as well as with the US Marshal Service."

Our federal government is undoubtedly one of the worst offenders in terms of developing a poor networking culture. The siloed mainstream Republicans are not engaging with the siloed Democrats. Neither is engaging effectively with those in the Tea Party silo.

The silo culture in DC is strangling America's ambitions and efforts to continue to be great. America needs new leadership, and Washington needs a new, dramatically better culture.

Law and accounting firms often work in silos. Law and accounting firms with diversified practice areas, regardless of being a single or a multiple-locations firm, have their profitable growth stunted and the careers of many of their highest potential professionals dampened because they do not have a winning networking and relationship development–focused culture. They manage their businesses in silos and in layers.

Too often the heads of the various practice areas don't talk and bond with each other, so cross selling among practice areas just doesn't happen. Leaders of the multiple offices don't communicate effectively, so there is limited sharing of ideas, best practices, and cross selling geographically. Various levels within the firm don't talk and get to know each other.

Internal friendships are vital to developing successful results-producing cultures. The new recruits, the staff lawyers or accountants, the CPA managers or senior lawyers, and partners seldom, if ever, meet and get to know each other well both professionally and personally. So internal mentoring is not happening sufficiently.

Professionals get frustrated. In tough times, they put in an adequate effort but don't go the extra mile. In better times, turnover is high with the best performers moving on, looking for a better culture where networking efforts aimed at driving profitable business growth and accelerating individual careers will be appreciated and rewarded.

In Search of a Better Culture

Recently I had eggs with a good friend and a partner generating about $1 million in fees annually in a metro NY law firm with twenty-five attorneys. A few years previous, she had been with the firm when it was headed by a former general partner she just didn't respect. She had been miserable there. At the first opportunity, she joined another quality regional firm as a partner for a few years. She remained until her previous law firm recruited her back when the former general partner retired.

Twelve months later, I was shocked at her answer when I asked her how she was doing back at her old firm. I had not seen her since she made that move a year or so ago.

"I hate it. I can't wait to leave. A couple of us are thinking about starting our own practice," she told me.

It was hard to imagine how terrible the culture was under the new leader who reneged on many of the promises he made to recruit her back. In addition, there apparently is little transparency in the firm. My friend cannot even get access to accurate accounting records documenting fees she generates for the firm and on which part of her compensation is based.

Earlier this year, the general partner spent over $400,000 of firm funds, claiming it was spent redoing his office and parts of the rest of the office. My friend suspects, because there has not been an open discussion of the costs, that some of the remodeling money actually went into upgrading the senior partner's home!

With a culture this corrupt, the firm cannot possibly survive. I am in the process of helping my friend and another partner with the firm develop a plan for exiting to create their own competitive practice.

Why Not Get the Receptionist Business Cards?

Recently I was visiting the New York office of a national law firm trying to get them as a business development client. While waiting for my meeting with the partner who would have a big part in making the decision to use or not use us, I started talking with the receptionist who had a mind-boggling great smile and personality.

In minutes I learned her name, found out she had been with the firm seven years and lived in and commuted from the Poconos in Eastern Pennsylvania. She took a 5:15 a.m. bus every morning and seldom got home before nine. She was married with two kids and loved music. I happen to know a terrific place for jazz in the Poconos—Deer Head Inn—which I told her about and suggested maybe one night she and her husband could meet me and my wife there. She got all excited, so I gave her my business card and asked for hers so we could connect near term and arrange to try the Deer Head Inn together. She didn't have a business card.

The law firm had reached out to us for possible help coaching their people to drive revenue growth by doing a better networking and relationship development job. The firm's revenues were down. Salaries were being frozen. Some partners' bonuses were being whacked. Other expenses were being trimmed. Perks were being scaled back. Some of the better performers were leaving. Worst of all, some of their long-standing clients were sending some or all of their law work to more nimble, lower cost, equally high-quality lawyers.

Giving the receptionist her own business cards (after seven years with the firm) would not have solved any of these problems. But investing $25 at Vista Print so she could have five hundred of her own business cards would not have hurt anything or anybody at the firm. It certainly would have made her feel a bit more like she belonged in and was valued by the firm.

Assume the receptionist rides the bus to and from New York about 250 times a year with each trip taking about three hours, and assume she generally talks to the people sitting next to her. Also assume some portion of the other bus riders sitting next to her have reasonably important positions in the city with organizations her firm would like to be serving. Some of the other riders probably have some legal issues with which they are dealing.

It would not have hurt if she could talk intelligently about her firm and hand her fellow riders one of her business cards with pride. I am guessing just this simple little action of giving a key employee business cards would have made her feel more engaged and more valued at the firm. It is easily conceivable that this little gesture would have resulted in some additional work for the firm or maybe a new recruit or a strategic alliance or two.

To top it off, when I did meet the partner heading the New York office of this twenty-five office, 1,200-member national law firm, I steered the conversation around to the receptionist. I started by complimenting him for having such a positive, high-energy person working the front desk and being the first person that clients and potential clients talk to when they call or meet when they walk in.

I then asked him her name. He had no idea. I asked him where she lived. He had no clue but guessed Brooklyn, Queens, or maybe the Bronx. I asked him what time he thought she left home every day to get to work. Again, clueless. When I asked if the firm provides business cards to support staff like receptionists and admin assistants, he said no, firmly. I guess taking some pride in being fiscally smart!

To this day I am certain this high-powered law partner with his blue-blooded, Ivy League education and background and lead role helping to manage a decaying national firm has no idea of how damning is his lack of interest in at least one of his most important support staff people. I suspect this is the same attitude he has toward most of the other nonpartners in his silo-ossified organization.

Here's a question to consider. If you have people working in your organization who are not worthy of having a $25 box of simple business cards, why are they working there? Why shouldn't everyone in your organization have their own business cards?

Universities and Colleges Too Often Are Stuck Operating in Silos

Recently I have been working with universities and colleges, many under intense pressure from students and their parents who are no longer willing and able to afford escalating tuition costs and being more and more skeptical about the real value of a college degree, particularly from a "me too" institution. Enrollment on many campuses (not Harvard, Princeton, Stanford, MIT, and other high-end universities) is down dramatically.

Many long-standing universities have been closing their doors permanently. For example, Sweet Briar, an all-women's college founded in 1901, announced in March 2015 that it would be shutting down at the end of the academic year. That June, newspapers reported that motivated alumni were getting together to raise funding to keep the doors open. We'll see. One of the reasons cited for Sweet Briar's declining enrollment problems is the fact that they have been educating in a single silo—women students only. That has been a key component of their brand for well over a hundred years. Today young people no longer want to attend a single-sex university. If Sweet Briar is refinanced, part of the new development strategy will almost certainly involve admitting male students.

Yet university and college leaders are failing to develop a transparent, all-hands-on-deck culture to effectively tackle the key issues facing our educational institutions. They don't see the need either to teach their students networking and relationship development skills or to foster a networking and relationship development culture that embraces everybody associated with the institution including students, faculty, parents of students, administrators, alumni, suppliers, and others. Why don't universities give students business cards the first day they are on campus? Wouldn't having all of their students walking around handing out the college business cards and essentially acting like mobile billboards be a good thing?

Universities are no better than the majority of corporations and professional firms. Most too are stuck in their silos, not talking and sharing ideas and resources with each other. The head of the business school, for example, is not routinely talking with the head of the med school or the journalism school. None of them are typically communicating effectively with the alumni or with the students or students' parents or even with the administrators. Tenure doesn't help the situation any.

Can you imagine the power that would be unleashed within colleges and universities if the silos came down and open communication flowed and real relationships based on sharing ideas, trust, confidence, and friendship took root. It is scary to think about all the good things that would result in our education system.

And yet colleges and universities have not recognized the fact that they need to be teaching networking at all levels, to everybody in their entire organization. For students it should be a core course required to graduate. For everyone else, it should be a learning opportunity that will enrich all of their lives and help drive the success of the institution. Faculty success too often at the university level is heavily a function of generating grant funding, writing published white papers, and doing research—three important skills that unfortunately provide little networking training or experience.

It's no wonder colleges professors almost never think about coaching their students on these critical networking and relationship building life skills. Most faculty members do not know how to use these tools for their own advantage.

The penalties for the university and college silos to remain intact are huge. Students leave without key skills they need to find jobs and build robust careers. Many go unemployed or underemployed for long periods. So they feel cheated by their college education. Alumni support drifts lower. Future admissions will continue to creep or plunge lower with only a fraction of the university's total community addressing the threat and sharing ideas for reversing the situation. Costs will escalate because nobody is sharing best practices for developing innovative new services, programs, and technologies for containing costs. Progress developing a digital online component to their education platform will drag or never happen while online competition comes roaring down the pike, often from for-profit colleges and universities.

Is the University Killing Its Business School?

I met a couple of years ago with the dean of the business school of a prominent East Coast university best known for its science and technology programs. The business school has nearly a thousand students in total including undergraduates and graduates and is capable of handling an additional five hundred. Naturally the president and provost were concerned and applying pressure on the dean to increase total business school enrollment.

When I poked around during our discussion about ways the dean was trying to close this student gap, which I estimate represents about $20 million annually in lost admissions revenues as well as future alumni support, I asked how often he and his team go into state-based or regional high schools to recruit. Surprisingly, he said he never makes high school visits, but the university's admission team has frequent high school meetings throughout the region and throughout the year. The problem is they seldom talk about the business school, preferring instead to talk about (i.e., "sell") the university's core strength, which is delivering a high-quality science and technology education.

It was obvious to me that the silo mentality was inhibiting the university's marketing and development of their entire portfolio of quality education offerings. Besides dragging down the business school's total enrollment, I am guessing that many of the faculty and students in the business school feel a bit like second-class citizens because of the university's compartmentalized way of operating.

To solve the problem, which is certainly solvable, it's clear all the key leaders at the university have to develop a culture that encourages and rewards effective cross selling of all of their educational offerings. Along the East Coast are literally dozens of quality universities offering quality undergraduate and graduate business school programs (MIT, Harvard, Yale, Cornell, Columbia, NYU, Fordham, Rutgers, U Penn, Temple, Georgetown, and many others). It's a fiercely competitive market for faculty members, students, financial support, and corporate recruiting.

I suspect as long as the marketing efforts of the university are concentrated in a few silos, the business school will continue to stagnate and may even eventually disappear.

It's now late 2015, and my friend the dean is no longer head of the business school. He has moved on to other opportunities and has been replaced by an "interim" dean. I doubt the enrollment issue has been solved. The dean was not the issue. The university's culture was, and I suspect it still is.

Nashville and the country music industry and the thoroughbred racing industry are polar opposites when it comes to their cultures.

As I am wrapping up writing this book, American Pharoah has already won racing's first Triple Crown in over thirty-five years (the Kentucky Derby, the Preakness, and the Belmont). On the days when each race was being run, I was in my car heading to meetings, trying to find a radio station broadcasting the races. I had no luck. That sums up what I think of the thoroughbred racing industry's culture. When a true fan like me cannot listen to the industry's top races on national radio, then I would say the industry's culture is broken badly, probably way beyond repair.

I spent years in both thoroughbred racing as a fan when I was young and then later as a serious and successful breeder, owner, and trainer. I also spent years in the country music industry as a co-founder and publisher of Country Music magazine, by far the nation's leading magazine for fans and one that was published for over thirty years.

I have deep hands-on experience in both industries and can say without reservation that the culture of the country music industry, particularly in Nashville, is strong and healthy and generating results. There are lots of stakeholders in the country music industry including performers, their managers, the record labels, the studios, venues like the Grand Ole Opry and the clubs in Nashville and elsewhere, the musical instrument manufacturers, the Country Music Hall of Fame, radio stations playing country, songwriters, and the major Annual Country Music Awards TV shows. To varying degrees, the stakeholders talk and learn to work with each other, have solid relationships with each other, and generally pull together with the same core objectives: create great music, develop big stars, and build the international audience. There is more than enough money to spread around to keep everybody working hard and playing nicely in the sandbox.

The thoroughbred racing industry is quite a different situation altogether. Almost nobody communicates, nor works effectively with each other. The jockeys, many from outside the United States and with poor English language skills, are truly skilled athletes and interesting people but play virtually no role in helping promote and develop the industry. The various states with racing have conflicting regulations, particularly when it comes to medications available for use with race horses. Tracks around the country play little attention to major races taking place elsewhere, so often a major race at one track goes off at the same time as a major race is running at another track, making it virtually impossible for any of the few remaining dedicated fans to bet via online wagering and watch both races live on TVG, the cable channel covering the industry.

Your Culture at Home and Work is Critical.
It's Amazing What You Can Accomplish Over Eggs

Owners are constantly under financial pressure. The economics of the racing industry make it tough to breakeven as an owner. Few owners make a profit. Most are in it for the love of the sport. Owners have little leverage when it comes time to get their fair piece of the TV fees paid to tracks and of the betting dollars at the track and online. Their only viable action to force negotiations would be to withhold entering their horses. That's not realistic with the daily cost of maintaining a horse at a major race track being hundreds of dollars.

At one point I was deeply involved in racing. I was elected president of the organization representing owners and trainers in New Jersey (New Jersey Horsemen's Benevolent & Protective Association). I was also on the board of the national organization (HBPA) representing members nationwide. Nothing substantial has happened in a good way since I exited the thoroughbred racing industry. Press and media coverage generally is way down since the good old days.

At a minimum, the racing industry needs a commissioner of racing like all the other professional sports have such as football, baseball, basketball, hockey, tennis, and golf. The industry needs effective coordinated leadership. Unfortunately it won't happen. Too many silos are being protected.

Ten years from now, I expect country music will be still booming and the races we watch on TV, if any, will be broadcast on cable from Hong Kong, Australia, or Japan. The American thoroughbred racing industry, as we know it, will no longer exist. The culture will have killed it.

The Killion Extruders company I bought and ran had culture issues too. When my dad had a heart attack and passed away, he left a company with heavy-duty financial issues. For a bunch of reasons, I bought and decided to turn around the company, which, at the time, had under $1 million in sales and only ten to twelve employees working in a single small building in Verona, New Jersey.

The culture was poor. My dad ran it like a tough old-time boss would. He lacked a successor. The workers clocked in and out on a time clock and got paid by the hour with small annual raises. If people didn't like the culture, they could quit. If my dad didn't like a particular person, he would fire them. There was no transparency at all. My dad worked in the business and not on the business.

When I assumed leadership for the company, the day after my dad passed, I made some short-term changes that improved the culture and, as expected, boosted the productivity of the workforce almost immediately. I eliminated the time clock and put everyone on salary. It was important to me to trust the employees and for them to know that I did trust them. I created a profit-sharing bonus program and beefed up the benefits plan. I started having weekly morning coffee meetings to update everyone on how the company was doing.

In the early days of my taking charge, the employees feared the company would shut down with my dad no longer involved to hold it together. Most important of all, after buying the company, I gave fifty percent of my equity to one of the employees, the one who had the biggest upside and who had been with my dad the longest. Shortly thereafter, I created a stock option plan that covered many in the current and future leadership group. Plus the company continued some of the good things my dad did to support his version of a successful culture—for example, he gave turkeys away at Thanksgiving and wine at Christmas and hams at Easter to all the employees. These things may seem small now, but back then they had an important, positive impact on morale and on the culture.

As we improved the company and got it back on stable financial footing, we grew by moving from a small, single-floor building in Verona, New Jersey, to a much larger, three-story facility in Cedar Grove, New Jersey. We built a new manufacturing and engineering facility in West Palm Beach, Florida, that my partner headed. We opened three separate stand-alone laboratory facilities in New Jersey, Florida, and California. We put the labs into a new company we formed, Killion Extruders Development Inc.

With this spread-out infrastructure, we had to work particularly hard to develop a winning culture that fostered networking, teamwork, and relationship building among the people and with key strategic alliance organizations. Having three floors in the New Jersey facility with operations on the ground floor, engineering on the second floor, and management, accounting, sales, and marketing on the third floor made communicating effectively in the New Jersey facility a challenge. I spent a lot of time just "walking around" and recommend against multifloor facilities, if you can avoid it.

Having two separate manufacturing and engineering facilities fifteen hundred miles apart made us work particularly hard to avoid the "them versus us" syndrome, which is never easy. Having three small laboratory operations in three different states all under a second company and all apart from the two main manufacturing facilities sometimes left these people feeling somewhat isolated and out of the loop.

My partner, Norm Brown, and I worked together successfully for over ten years with a simple handshake being the basis of the partnership. We never put together an agreement in writing, which may seem insane, but we liked, respected, and trusted each other. The partnership worked, and Killion Extruders was a successful turnaround until we sold the company. One key to the turnaround was that we were aware that we had to work hard to create a culture that would foster internal and external positive networking and create career development opportunities for all the employees.

Business is not the only guilty party. Our government is generally mummified in silos with a dysfunctional culture.

Who doesn't think our government has lost its way? It is gridlocked with the Republicans, their Tea Party wing, and the Democrats sticking to their silos and failing the American people horribly. It is amazing that we all stand for it. I am not sure what it is going to take to dramatically change and improve the situation so that the people we elect can get back together and come to a fair consensus on the critical factors that will help drive America forward. I am pessimistic.

We are all well aware of how inefficient our major law enforcement agencies are with the CIA frequently not talking and cooperating with the FBI and neither being particularly motivated to work with state and local authorities. We have all been learning about the dysfunctional cultures in the Secret Service and the Veterans Administration.

The media are steering the rest of us into our own little silos with the CNNs and Rush Limbaughs of the world all pulling us in their particular directions with their own partisan agendas.

Changing the culture of the government would be a daunting task with no quick fix. However, I would certainly like to get a bunch of smart people together and try. If we don't make things better soon, circumstances will get a lot tougher for America both at home and globally.

Transitioning the Culture

In all organizations, how can a winning culture develop that encourages networking and relationship development with the end goal being to drive the profitable growth of the business while providing great career opportunities for all of the people? I could and probably will write another book just on this topic, but to get you thinking, here are a few points:

The leaders of the organization, starting with the head, have to buy into the concept that an open culture promoting internal and external networking and relationship development, based on mutual trust and respect, fairness, and transparency, is critical and will be created. The leaders have to be committed to breaking down the silos and minimizing the layering effect.

Their "buy in" will show up in their own exceptional personal internal and external networking and relationship development efforts.

They will be pushing to add relevant training programs to the operating budget. They will openly encourage their people to submit networking-related expenses for reimbursement and to allocate some "work time" to conduct effective business-related networking.

Your Culture at Home and Work is Critical.
It's Amazing What You Can Accomplish Over Eggs

They will find ways to incorporate evaluating a potential new hire's networking interest, experience, and aptitude into the recruiting process, and they will include evaluation of these skills and efforts in a person's performance review.

The leader's own networking performance will be noticed internally. Does he or she take a professional, sincere interest in the receptionist and all the other support team members? Does the CEO talk to everyone he or she passes in the halls and on the elevator? Does this leader have lunch occasionally with some of the worker-bees in his or her company and not just with the partners or with the C-level executives? Is the chief executive consistently working to break down the silos and knock out the hierarchy barriers?

Resources have to be invested in the process to change the culture. People have to be provided tools to help them network and develop relationships. A little training and coaching will go a long way toward getting everyone thinking and acting the right way. It might not be a bad idea to buy one or two books on the topic to be given out internally during the holidays or as part of the performance review process.

Why not give everybody who has been with the organization six months or longer 500 business cards? Or better yet, do it the day they join the organization. Make them feel part of the team right away. Put the organization's logo, mission statement, website, or a significant customer quote on the back side so every card becomes a mini ad for the organization.

Make certain the organization has a viable system for capturing the names and contact data for every new business-relevant person met by members of the organization. Teach them to know who is or who is not a viable contact to be included in the organization's database. Show them how to get the names entered into the system. An organization's database of viable contacts is one of the most important assets any organization has. The goal should be to increase its value every day by constantly adding important new contacts and cleaning out the dead ones.

My experience is that, even in well-run organizations, the majority of people have no real idea how to use the company's contact management system. Too many organizations fail to appreciate how important their database of key contacts can be.

People within the organization should be encouraged to invest some business time in meeting new business-related people. They should also be encouraged to submit proper expenses that they incur meeting people on behalf of the organization. In many professional firms and corporations, I have seen experienced, solid people actually be afraid of being even thirty minutes late or leaving thirty minutes early occasionally to meet someone he or she thinks would have an interest in working with or being a new client or resource for the organization. Well over seventy-five percent of the people going through our networking coaching programs say they never submit networking-related expenses! That blows my mind.

Everybody within the organization needs to be encouraged to talk with everyone else within the organization, at every opportunity. I am astounded how often people walk around the halls of large organizations passing people with neither even saying hello. Often they actually look down to avoid eye contact. If you want to have some fun, when you are in an organization—yours or someone else's—start saying hello to everyone you encounter. You will be amazed how many people look just plain startled. That's not good. Try talking with people in a crowded elevator in a New York high rise office building.

There is hard evidence that people who have friends within an organization are significantly more productive than if they feel friendless. According to one Harvard study, people who initiate workplace friendships, and join in with work-related social activities, are forty percent more likely to receive promotions than those who don't.

Important people within the organization who need to have close working relationships with each other should have a firm, scheduled plan for meeting regularly. Breaking down the silos in an organization is unlikely to happen unless this occurs. Using a large accounting firm as an obvious example, I think the heads of the various practice areas (tax, audit, forensic accounting, risk management, compliance, and others) should meet regularly—let's say one evening a month, from 6 to 8:30 p.m. All sitting at one table over dinner sharing their latest successes, experiences, ideas, and challenges. It won't happen quickly, but eventually the skepticism, internal competition, defenses, and guards will come down to be replaced by trust, friendship, camaraderie, candor, and a deep and honest passion for helping each other.

Similarly, in a law firm with many practice areas, or at a university with many degree programs, or in a corporation with many important departments and divisions, the siloed leaders should meet at least once a month for two to three hours each time. Again, get them out of the office. Periodic meetings over dinner work well for team building. These informal sessions give everyone an opportunity to talk openly about their areas of responsibility, their challenges, their people, and their success stories. Asking for new, relevant contacts and sharing best practices works wonders. People learn to know each other, respect each other, care about each other, take an interest in each other, and want to help each other. These "bonding" dinners need to be required, not optional. They are enormously important.

My experience shows that this process may take up to a year to start to bear real fruit. However, when the barriers come down and the trust factor goes up, the opportunities of all kinds, including cross selling, will flow.

One word of caution: For this process to work, the conversation around the table has to include everyone participating equally and as equals. If the discussions are dominated by one or two people, the benefits won't be there. Sometimes, organizations bring in facilitators to make certain the meetings do in fact build great trust, chemistry, and rapport. I have played this role in the past.

Effective teamwork at the highest level in an organization will set the right example for everyone else on the team. The silo leaders will make certain that this cross pollination among the various units also happens further down in the organization.

In one major international accounting firm that retained our firm to coach their senior women professionals, at the end of our series of coaching workshops, several participants took it upon themselves to start holding monthly prework coffee discussions at a local shop just to keep the camaraderie and solid working relationships growing.

In a multi-office organization, a way has to be found to bring the office heads together periodically with the same basic goal being to improve the culture and the relationships among the various offices' leaders. In an organization with multiple US offices, would it not be worth investing some T&E expenses to bring location heads together maybe six times a year for a couple of days (Friday and Saturday would work) in an effort to develop trust, friendships, and shared knowledge, goals, and hurdles? Do you doubt that the organization would perform better if the key leaders were all on the same page and working as an integrated team with less friction among them hampering innovation and teamwork?

Similarly, for international organizations, do you think there would be major benefits from finding ways to bring country leaders together in person more frequently with the goal being to strengthen the personal and professional relationships among them?

After we sold Killion Extruders to UK-based Thermal Scientific, I joined the parent company's board of directors. We shortly thereafter started having quarterly progress review and strategy development in two-day meetings in the United States for the leaders of the US-based companies that had been acquired by Thermal Scientific. Similar quarterly meetings were held in Europe for the European companies in the Thermal Scientific quiver.

Twice a year the board hosted a two-day program in Bamford, UK, for leaders of all the companies regardless of their locations. These meetings were enormously helpful building a winning culture for Thermal Scientific, a public company that grew impressively both organically and via acquisitions. Three years after we sold Killion Extruders to Thermal Scientific, the parent company was acquired at a healthy premium to the public share price by Tube Industries, a large public UK company.

Should the recruiting of new talent always take into account the recruits' potential ability to network, develop solid relationships, and drive profitable growth? Why not? Given two candidates interested in joining your organization and having similar backgrounds and similar apparent job-related skills, wouldn't you rather bring aboard the one you conclude is going to be much more effective networking and helping to grow the business?

Most young staff members are recruited into most organizations without ever having any training in networking and relationship building. For the first few years, these gaps in their training do not show up as they spend the bulk of their time doing the grunt work required early in their career. But as they mature within the organization and start to think about their long-term career opportunities, the "powers to be" start talking to them about the need for them to start generating new business and other opportunities for the organization if they hope to crack into the partner or C-level group—that is, break through the "skills ceiling." Many of these professionals with eight to ten years of experience look like deer in the headlights when they are suddenly confronted with the unanticipated expectation that they are now expected to start bringing in new business and creating other important benefits. They simply have no idea of what to do.

It clearly would be much better and much fairer to make this point right from the first hiring decision: "If you hope to make partner or become a key executive within our organization, you eventually will be expected to be a revenue generator and someone who impacts our successful growth. Are you prepared to make the effort required to be an effective rainmaker?"

The NQ Pulse (introduced in chapter 2) developed as a proprietary tool by Bluestone+Killion for assessing these aptitudes is one way to get a reading on a person's current ability to network effectively.

Early in 2014 we held a three-hour networking workshop for

two hundred students at a prominent metro New York law school. Our goal was to help them start to develop the difference-making networking and relationship development tools they needed to find important internships while in law school and then to land attractive first jobs after graduating. The average NQ Pulse of these first- and second-year law students was in the low thirties, or less than half the skill level they needed. We were not surprised that many of them were struggling to land significant internships and first jobs out of law school.

Why not include some junior members of the team in key meetings? How can bright, high-potential, motivated young professionals be encouraged by being excluded from many of your organization's most important meetings? It happens all the time.

Wise clients will respect you for bringing junior-level, smart, talented people into important situations as real learning opportunities. Throughout my entire business career, I have made a practice of including young people in my key meetings. I have never encountered resistance from those we were meeting. More often they feel good about being included in the development of our young people.

Within the past month, I had breakfast with a recent college graduate in marketing who is interning in New York City with a large publishing company. She admitted she was not overly busy in this role. I asked her if she was invited to sit in on the various meetings the management team of this relatively small business unit had both internally and with current and potential clients. She admitted no. She was almost always excluded from participating in most meetings. Why? That boggles my little mind.

If a person is good enough to be recruited to your team, why are they not good enough to sit in on almost all meetings as long as they are staying current with their responsibilities and the meeting agenda is neither confidential nor particularly sensitive?

I love helping young people flourish and always make a point of including them in almost any meetings I have either internally or externally. I also find that most leaders in other organizations also relish having young, talented people sit in on meetings with them. Do you know any quality, experienced people who do not enjoy and want to help young people develop?

I like hiring college students as paid summer interns. I have been doing it for years. They always contribute and more than carry their share of the load. When I owned and was running Killion Extruders, I had a relatively large office, big enough for a couple of desks and a small conference table. Every summer I would put the intern at the other desk in my office so he or she could be part of almost every in-person and phone conversation meeting and discussion I had. How much of a learning experience do you think that was for the interns?

P.S.: I think interns should be paid. You won't work for nothing, so why should they? I do prefer to pay interns by revenue sharing on unique projects we tackle together. This gives them skin in the game and means they can earn far more that the typical $10 per hour if our revenue-generating project is successful. In the end, however, we always pay them fairly, even if our jointly generated revenues fall short of our goal. At the outset, I just like to get them sharing responsibility for our combined efforts to drive profitable revenues.

Finally, it makes sense to have a compensation system that recognizes success generating new business and adding to the organization's profitable growth in other ways. That seems obvious, but it is not done effectively in many organizations. I am not a compensation expert, but there are plenty of capable consultants in this space if you need some guidance. I know that developing the "right" incentive compensation system is not easy. What works in one organization may not work in another, but finding a way to reward people contributing new revenue-generating and other business development and improvement opportunities can be important.

It's also important to recognize that just having an incentive system may not provide strong enough incentives to network and develop revenue-generating relationships.

Improving a Law Firm's Culture

We coached everyone working in a single office, sharply focused family law firm. They have four owner-partners and twenty nonpartner attorneys plus some administrative support staff. The partners were frustrated that only the partners had ever generated substantial new client assignments. Even then it was primarily three of the four partners who drove the revenue growth of the firm. None of the twenty nonpartner attorneys, with extensive career experience, had ever brought in a single piece of new business, which is hard to even imagine.

At a meeting with the partners, I poked around to learn about the incentive system. They said they pay fifteen percent of any new client revenues brought in by "anyone" in the firm. I asked if this included their exceptional receptionist and talented controller and other support staff members. I also asked if they provided business cards to the nonprofessional support members of their team. Their answer to both questions was no. They had never considered including these people in any form of incentive or bonus compensation system and had certainly never thought about giving them business cards. And yet, with a fifty percent divorce rate in America, when it comes to turning up potential family law work, why isn't the receptionist or the controller with their family and community contacts just as likely to learn of a potential new client contact with family issues as is a nonpartner attorney or a partner?

We started unleashing the potential in this firm by getting everyone business cards, including everyone in various forms of an incentive and year-end bonus system, and including everyone in the business development workshops we conducted. All of their people learned how to effectively network, create new win-win relationships, and be sensitive to spotting opportunities for the firm to serve their personal contacts who are dealing with challenging family issues.

Now taking responsibility for successfully growing the practice is a total team effort. Everyone has been given financial incentives and the training and tools needed to grow their personal and professional networks and spot business development opportunities. The culture has been strengthened.

Every organization has a culture. Some are deliberately and carefully developed and managed. Others evolve without much deliberation or leadership. In either case the "buck stops here" concept applies—that is, an organization's culture in the long run really reflects the leadership at the top. Organizations with outstanding cultures will always outperform those with weaker cultures.

Early in 2015, I had the privilege of sitting in on a discussion about the global leading company Ferrero founded in the 1940s in Italy. You know the still privately owned company I am sure through two of their leading consumer brand products: Nutella, the chocolate hazel nut spread and Tic Tacs. The discussion was being led by the President of Nutella, USA. When asked point-blank what accounted for the international company's exceptional, global, consistently profitable growth, he never hesitated with his two-word answer: our culture. In 2009 Ferrero was honored by the Reputation Institute of New York as being the world's most reputable company. Culture does matter.

Network: All the Time, Everywhere With Everyone

Chapter Twelve

Now What?
Develop Your Networking Action Plan

Networking and developing significant relationships is all about generating potentially new opportunities that lead to important results. If there is not a clear purpose to your networking efforts, then you will just be spinning your wheels, simply meeting people (often not the highest potential ones) and without much to show for the effort. Your life is too short for that.

To achieve anything meaningful, as a result of your "serious" networking, you need to have specific networking goals, a well-defined networking action plan, and accountability.

When developing your written action plan, it makes sense to have three stages: a one-month plan; a three-month plan; and a six-month plan. Maybe one could be a twelve-month plan if your goals stretch that far. But I suggest you develop a habit of planning your networking efforts starting with shorter-term, more manageable goals and actions steps.

Approaching the plan development in stages allows you to set interim goals that you can target to accomplish in tighter time frames.

When developing your plans you need to:

• Define your goal(s), which may be career, business, or personally oriented or a combination of all three. Be specific setting these.

• Make a note of how many hours a week you will spend networking to accomplish your goals. Most people serious about developing a substantial career should network at least five hours a week minimum on an ongoing basis. More would be better.

• For the one-month plan, list the specific people or types of people you will network with in the next thirty days who can help you accomplish your goals.

• Also, for the one-month plan, list the various ways you will strengthen your Internet presence including improving your LinkedIn profile. You need to keep making this online profile more and more robust and keep it timely and accurate.

• For the three- and six-month plans, list other specific people or types of people you will target to network within these time frames. Also list your clusters of contacts that you will explore the most for important relationships. For pursuing longer-term goals, you may not know the specific people you need to reach. However, you certainly can identify the types of people you need to target.

• Identify the important events you will go to or create in these time periods.

• Identify any groups you will join or consider starting in these periods. Think broadly about these options.

The same template can be used for each plan or you can roll all the plans together in the one template, which is my preference. You may in fact have multiple action plans, each with their own specific goals and action steps. For example, you may have:

• A family goal of getting your son or daughter into a good college that fits their abilities and ambitions.

• A personal goal of finding a new career opportunity.

• A goal of starting or buying your own business or raising funding for an existing business might be a goal to be accomplished through networking.

• A goal of being promoted to a higher position within your firm and raising your income substantially.

Regardless of your end objectives, you need to develop a networking and relationship development action plan that will help you accomplish them. The plan needs to be in writing. I think, to keep the pedal to the metal, start with a networking action plan covering the next six months, broken into thirty-day, three-month, and six-month increments and then plan to assess progress, change it appropriately, and wind up with a second six-month plan, if necessary.

To go along with your networking action plan, you need a workable system for maintaining a database of the contacts that you develop in this process. Obviously you also need a method for following up with people in a priority order.

If building your brand is part of your plan, then you might also include the publications you would like to write for and the groups you will target for future speaking engagements.

Share your action plan with another person or maybe with two or three other people and then meet with them periodically to review your progress and get their input.

What is even better, team up with another person or two equally committed to developing and executing their own networking action plan so that you can be accountable to each other as you move ahead.

In our networking coaching sessions, when we get to the point of participants' developing their networking action plans, we always try to pair them up with another in the group and have them commit to working together with this process in the future.

In our coaching programs, at some point our work with the client organization ends. For our coaching to develop real teeth, we need to have the participants be accountable to themselves and possibly to each other for implementing what they learn from our coaching.

To reemphasize, successful, results-producing networking can be done by anyone. These are skills that can be learned. The more you work at networking, the better you will become. Having a written networking action plan will be helpful in pulling together your thinking regarding what you want to accomplish and who can make that happen for you.

The more robust your network of relevant people you connect with, the richer will be every personal and professional aspect of your life. So you are encouraged to successfully network all the time, everywhere with everybody. It will pay off for you, your family, your friends, and the organizations you work with. This book provides you with the guidance you can capitalize on to become proficient at developing and using these skills.

Networking Action Plan

This plan is for: [ ] 30 days [ ] 3 Months [ ] 6 Months

My Specific Networking Results Goals

1. _____   2. _____
3. _____   4. _____

Targeted Connections – Names or Types

1. _____   2. _____
3. _____   4. _____
5. _____   6. _____

Possible Events to Attend

1. _____   2. _____

Possible Groups to Join

1. _____   2. _____

Possible Publications to Write For

1. _____   2. _____
Possible Speaking Engagements

1. _____   2. _____

I will commit _____ hours per week to networking.

[ ] Yes, I will maintain a strong, current LinkedIn profile.

Network: All the Time, Everywhere With Everyone

Acknowledgments

I owe thanks to the people who took time to review my manuscript and provide their feedback, which is included under testimonials. Thank you.

Like in all families, my parents, Fred and Laurie Killion, played a major role in shaping me. They were my role models as they battled through difficult times following the Great Depression, supported only by their grammar school educations, wits, energy, and will to "make it." Obviously their willingness to sacrifice personally so I could attend great universities was huge. My dad's fierce entrepreneurial effort to launch and grow his own business is part of my DNA for which I will forever be grateful. He taught me the value and importance of showing up every day, always trying your best, being willing to take risks, following your interests and passions, being self-reliant, thinking bigger, and never quitting. One of his strengths was his strong people skills. People liked him, and he could generally develop a successful relationship with anybody.

My mom taught me the importance of family and the role of parents in helping their kids go further than they themselves ever imagined. She in particular emphasized the importance of a good education, which neither of my parents had an opportunity to pursue.

Obviously I owe thanks to Sandra Wendel who heads her own editing and writing firm, Write On, Inc., which is based in Omaha, Nebraska. I was networked to Sandra for editorial services by Lynn

Evans, a good friend and Certified Financial Planner who heads her own financial advisory firm and who had worked with Sandra on her own important book project, Power of the Purse, that was published in 2015. It's a significant financial resource for women wanting and needing to take more effective charge of their financial futures. Sandra is the successful coauthor along with Mayo Clinic's Dr. Edward T. Creagan of How Not to Be My Patient.

I also owe thanks to Opemipo Sokan and Walter Franks, two young graphic designers and web developers who worked with me to design and get the book ready for printing and to develop www.networkallthetime.com. Fairleigh Dickinson University's Janet O'Neill referred me to them—thus again showing the power of networking.

The thousands of people I have met over the years deserve special thanks for helping me learn, grow, and develop my strong networking and relationship development skills. For the most part, they have been patient as I continuously sharpened my ability to ask thought-provoking questions in an ongoing search to find the common "finger holds" that lead to long-term, results-producing, extraordinary friendships as well as personal and career development relationships, one of life's vital skills for all of us

Finally, I owe most of what I have accomplished to Judy Chapman (Killion), the teenage girl I met in Caldwell High School. Six decades later, we are still together. She has been my bedrock. Of course, our son, Jonathan, is owed my special thanks for being such a great son, always at my side offering encouragement and, in recent years, providing his wisdom and guidance as he lived with Judy and me through the entrepreneur's roller coaster career we have relished. Judy and I remember one of Jonathan's comments at the dinner table when he was quite young: "Don't you guys ever talk about anything other than business?"

About the Author

Jack Killion developed and used his networking abilities to accelerate his career, which has included starting and growing profitable businesses, providing guidance, while working with McKinsey & Company, to business owners of all sizes including Fortune 500s, and advising boards of corporations and nonprofits.

He has successfully multitasked over the years to start and own seven different successful businesses in venture capital, magazine and book publishing, industrial equipment manufacturing, thoroughbred horse breeding and racing, real estate development, hedge fund investing, and executive coaching.

Currently he heads the fourteen-year-old Eagle Rock Diversified Fund, a fund-of-funds, and is cofounder of the three-year-old Bluestone+Killion firm that coaches business leaders to network and develop results-producing relationships. He is a trustee with his wife's Garden State Woman Education Foundation, a 501(c)(3) that provides scholarship and mentoring support and organizes business and STEM and leadership summit events for high school girls.

He also advises entrepreneurs looking for his input on raising funding and developing and executing strategic development plans. In this role he is focusing on helping develop PeopleProductive as a game-changing new business focused on helping diverse organizations drive increased productivity and performance by assessing, monitoring, and improving their cultures.

In the past three years he has coached over two thousand difference-making corporate leaders and professionals to accelerate their careers, drive their business growth, and enrich their lives by sharpening their networking and relationship development skills. His clients have been with accounting and law firms, diverse corporations, financial services firms, universities, and charities.

Early in his career Jack worked full-time for a French manufacturing company in France and for a British tech company in the United Kingdom. He traveled extensively using his networking abilities to create opportunities for his various businesses on a global basis including Eastern and Western Europe, China, and throughout Latin America.

Jack earned his bachelor's degree in mechanical engineering from Yale University and his master's from MIT's Sloan School of Management.

He has taught for over twenty-five years in the undergraduate and graduate business school programs at Rutgers, Montclair State, and Fairleigh Dickinson universities. He was named the first Entrepreneur in Residence at Fairleigh Dickinson.

Jack has served for over fifteen years as an educational counselor for MIT, interviewing high school students applying to MIT. He also is the organizer, at MIT's request, of a networking group for New Jersey–based graduates of MIT's Sloan School of Business.

Jack is a frequent guest speaker and writes often on topics related to networking, relationship development, and organizational cultures for a variety of business publications including Citi's blog, New York Enterprise Report, and the New York Law Journal.

He has tapped into his extensive network to organize over two hundred successful events globally on diverse topics including financial and health-related programs for women, wireless and mobile communications conferences for corporate end users, networking programs for clients and potential clients, magazine publishing conferences, and polymer processing conferences.

He has networked his way into important strategic alliances

with leaders of universities, federal and state government agencies, and other corporations and professional firms.

He served in the US Army as the primary military support to the head of the army's global metrology and calibration mission.

Jack lives with Judy and works from a home office on his fifty-acre Walnut Farm and, when not working, enjoys traveling, finding exceptional out-of-the way restaurants, reading extensively, and mentoring young people and adults in transition. He is writing his next book to share his entrepreneurial experiences with others who have stepped off the ledge to start and grow their own businesses.

Network with Jack Killion at:

Jack@networkallthetime.com, (908) 507-9879, or via the website at www.networkallthetime.com.

Made in USA - North Chelmsford, MA
1078928_9780996671705
04.14.2020 0717